Seeing Beyond Saint Louis

Elsah

Barringer Fifield with Keith Recker

Seeing Beyond Saint Louis

Photographs by Herb Weitman

Published by Washington University
Campus Stores
Saint Louis, Missouri

First printing

Library of Congress Catalog Card Number: 90-071204
ISBN 0-9623809-1-1

Printed in the United States of America

 BOOKS & BOOKS

are published by
Washington University Campus Stores
St. Louis, Missouri

Acknowledgments

Debts are not supposed to be happy things. But those we incurred in the course of preparing this book are all owed to people of such wit and kindness that we could only wish for more.

A number of people in St. Louis were unstinting in providing counsel and information. They include Gertrude Bernoudy, Jim Van Sant, Maggie Stearns, Charles Mackay, Thomas Danisi, Carol Miller, Mrs. Wilbur M. Finger, Pat McCain, Lowell M. Zuck, Ben Van Driver, Donald Wilson, and Roy Ledbetter. Tom Hall gave us the sort of practical guidance girded with true wisdom he was famous for.

Esley Hamilton never let us down. Both his published work and his words of advice were invaluable. Carl Ekberg's superb scholarship and unselfishness likewise were without price.

Nicholas Burckel and Jim MacDonald each made available very useful books, as did the excellent Missouri Historical Society staff.

Outside St. Louis we were fortunate to encounter the help of Judy Bauer, Juanita Holst, Shirley Myers, Kay Dunne, Charlotte Ballard, and the Schultes of Dutzow.

Natalie Villmer, Rick Zoellner, and Carol Pfitzinger all showed us their faith in their works; we will not forget their amiability. Alan Maes, Alice Widmer, and Krista Wibskov were similarly helpful.

Clara Fieselmann gave us a sense of the soul of Gasconade County that will always remain with us. Paul Williams, as graciously, showed the secrets of Bonne Terre.

Charles Hosmer and Charles Lockwood each gave

pertinent assistance, as did John Herold, Susan Denny, and Mike Skele.

Emily Pulitzer and Mark and Patricia Schulte gave thoughtful readings to the manuscript. Their interest has been a mighty support.

Debby Aronson, Jim Burmeister, William Cornelius, Nancy Galofré, Liesl Heeter, Jo Olson Scheffel, and Barbara Volkmann also read it and had many useful suggestions.

Brooke and Bill Recker's help was both deft and thoroughgoing; we will always be grateful for it.

Finally, we will never have a more convincing editor nor truer moral support than Trudi Spigel.

Sandy Creek covered bridge

We dedicate this book to our magnanimous friend, Bill Gleason.

Contents

Church of the Holy Family, Cahokia

Introduction

This is a book about exotic places. Even people whose jobs depend on them are often unfamiliar with the St. Louis region's attractions. One tourism official, hearing about the sites we were looking at in her area, was downright incredulous. "You're really interested in those podunks cattywampus from nowhere?"

We were and — after an average of five circuits of each of the following itineraries — we still are. Not only did we not get bored, the podunks appealed to us more and more. For St. Louis is a blessed spot; few cities' environs offer such varied riches.

As remarkable as the hamlets frozen in time, the enchanting landscapes, the noble farmsteads, is the region's historical wealth. Moral giants — Mother Duchesne, Daniel Boone, General Grant — have sojourned here. Cultural dramas — survival of French and German ways — have been played out here. Religious striving — especially Lutheran and Catholic — has found expression here.

The tours, even those with an esoteric or didactic edge, have all been designed principally as pleasant outings. That meant excluding places interesting in themselves, but not easily worked into an agreeable day trip. Jefferson City and Springfield both come to mind. Some of the longer trips are even too rich; you may want to prune them when time is limited.

The official state road maps are useful. In some complicated spots, however, our written directions are indispensable. We frequently note exact mileage from one point to another; if you glance ahead in the text you will know when to zero your trip odometer. All this is easier, of course, if the driver is accompanied by a navigator.

The tours link sites related by history as well as by geography. It was history that dictated that the first itinerary take us southward in Illinois; there the region's earliest European settlement took place. It seemed rational then to follow the points of the compass clockwise, ending the long tours with a trip north on the Mississippi's east bank.

Arrival is not what these tours are about; the pleasure of the cumulative experience outshines the single sites' historical or artistic importance. Here more than elsewhere, perhaps, the trip is in the traveling.

Telephone numbers for the sites are given at the conclusion of each chapter. Visitors may want to check hours before starting out, since they change, as do admission prices.

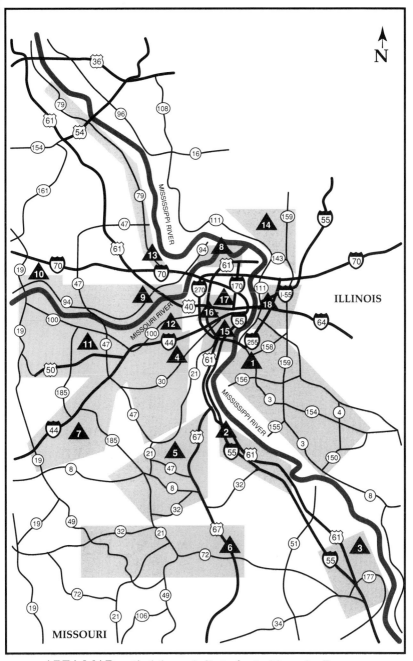

AREA MAP — *Shaded areas indicate chapter itineraries. For driving directions, consult the text.*

Courthouse, Cahokia

Begins at U.S. 40/Interstate 64 and Illinois 3

Americans usually see their history as a determined
westward progression across a totally wild continent.
We tend to forget that when Daniel Boone blazed trails
into Kentucky in the 1770s, a string of displaced European communities already existed behind and to the
west of that wilderness: the outposts of colonial France.

The Atlantic, in colonial times, was dominated by the
English and the Spanish. In order to link their Canadian
to their Caribbean possessions the French turned to the
inland waterways, establishing missions, forts and commercial posts from Quebec to the Gulf of Mexico.

This tour is organized around that empire's vivid
remnants along the Mississippi. They remind us that, had
France rather than Britain won the French and Indian
War in 1763, America might have stretched not east-west
from sea to shining sea — but north to south, from frozen
tundra to balmy shore.

The first sight on our itinerary heading south on
Illinois 3 is French only in name. Sauget's industries are
as spectacular on the skyline as they are poisonous at the
waterline; the EPA called their effluents the most toxic in
a six-state area. Note the anthropomorphic chimneys
atop the rubber reclaiming plant opposite Cerro.

Continue south on Illinois 3 to nearby Cahokia. Here
the Abundant Love Church — like Sauget another sign of
our times — flashes messages such as, "It's easier to build

a boy than mend a man." Before you, on the left, is the thoroughly French vertical log Church of the Holy Family. Turn left toward it on Illinois 157.

From the outset Europeans came to the New World in search not only of riches, but also of souls; six missionary priests accompanied Columbus on his second voyage. Yet conversion and conquest did not always complement one another. Priests from Bartolomé de Las Casas in the sixteenth century to liberation theologians in the twentieth have protested abuse of America's native peoples.

Seventeenth-century Jesuits opposed Robert de La Salle for similar reasons. La Salle, having descended from the Great Lakes to the Gulf of Mexico in 1682, claimed the entire Mississippi Valley for France. The Jesuits had another sort of empire in mind. "They assert they are going to create a new Paraguay here," La Salle wrote, referring to the priests' utopian Indian protectorate in South America.[1]

But usually the French in America succeeded in combining the spiritual and the material. The great voyage of exploration preceding La Salle's was the 1673 one of Joliet, a trader, and Père Marquette, a Jesuit with a remarkable gift for Indian relations. Marquette's loving account of the indigenous inhabitants of the Illinois country made the region a kind of spiritual El Dorado for generations of French missionaries.

Old Cahokia was a typical product of French mingling of motives. In fact it was La Salle's lieutenant, the Neapolitan Henri de Tonti, who guided three priests of Quebec's Seminary of Foreign Missions here. They built a church and outbuildings in 1699, the year of Williamsburg's founding and almost twenty years before New Orleans'. The Seminarians chose Cahokia for its central position on the Mississippi, which would facilitate their work throughout the valley. The post soon had a commercial function in the Indian and fur trade as well.

Built one hundred years after the Seminarians' arrival, the Church of the Holy Family's *poteaux-sur-solle* construction — vertical posts on a sill — is classically creole. Worship was also creole-style, the antithesis of the dour proceedings common in Anglo-American religion. "The church was the great place of gay resort on Sundays and holidays, and the priest was the advisor and director and companion of all his flock." [2]

Notice the robust stone crucifix above the entrance, the well-placed diagonal corner supports, and the convincing simplicity of the whole. "Qui persevera jusqu' à la fin sera sauvé," says an inscription inside on the right wall. The church, third on this site, looks as though it will indeed "persevere unto the end, and be saved." There is a very old graveyard outside.

The 1807 Jarrot House just east has also shown staying power. One of the oldest brick structures in Illinois, its solidity has been tested by the constant flooding that carried away nearly all the rest of old Cahokia. Though in the Federal style, unusual for its time and place, it was built by an enterprising Frenchman, Nicholas Jarrot. His 25,000 acre holdings included what is now East St. Louis as well as the Lewis and Clark expedition's first campsite at the mouth of Wood River.

Jarrot and his wife, a Beauvais from Ste Genevieve, were known for their dancing parties, held in the second floor ballroom. They entertained Lafayette during his 1825 tour of America.

French conviviality was, along with the church, the impetus for town life. "The French population will not reside on farms each family to itself like the Americans. They always live in villages where they may enjoy their social pleasures. The church also induces them to live near it in villages," said John Reynolds, an early-nineteenth-century visitor.[3]

Cahokia's third creole building is the courthouse. Go south a few yards on Illinois 3 and turn right on Second Street. Built in 1737 as home of François Saucier, engineer of Fort de Chartres and surveyor of old Ste Genevieve, the vertical log structure became a courthouse in 1793. This was in response to the new American government's order that each county have a courthouse, county jail, pillory, whipping post, and stocks.

Floods prompted the removal of the county seat to Belleville in 1814. After various transformations, including a period as a tavern and subsequent appearances at Chicago's 1893 Columbian Exhibition and at St. Louis' 1904 World's Fair, the old building was reconstructed on its original site in 1939. The small house and its carefully chosen exhibits give a sense of the vitality of creole life in Illinois. We learn about creole economics, too. Seven doe skins or six muskrat pelts were worth one prime beaver pelt — which in turn bought one bottle of brandy.

Continuing south, Illinois 3 passes Dupo, whose name is an anglicized reduction of the old French village's *Prairie du Pont.* Nearby Indian mounds testify that even before its creole period, the area had a life as a satellite of the Cahokia Mounds community. Dupo too has a very old creole structure, the Boismenue house, recently discovered by the town's fire chief. It has not yet been restored.

Follow Illinois 3 south to Columbia, where a sign directs you left onto Main Street, which follows the old Kaskaskia Trail. Here stand a number of nineteenth-century houses, including the 1867 Greek Revival Gundlach-Grosse House at 625 North Main. The house's name suggests Columbia's ethnic makeup, a hint confirmed by the landmark Eberhard's Bavarian Stein Museum and Restaurant at 117 North Main. Germans began coming to this rich farming area in the 1830s; it was first settled by Anglo-Southerners at the end of the eighteenth century. Before rejoining Illinois 3 note tiny 928 South Main on the left.

Less than seven miles southward lies another German-American community, Waterloo. The Waterloo Winery at 725 North Market (which is Illinois 3) is one of many buildings on the National Register of Historic Places here. Turn right half a mile farther south for the Peterstown House on North Main Street. The Connecticut-style white frame dwelling was a stagecoach stop on the Kaskaskia Trail. Southward at Mill and Main note the Monroe County Courthouse. Make a right onto Mill. You'll pass Sts. Peter and Paul, built in 1883; it has a noble interior and good stained glass windows. There is a delicate iron fence in front of the rectory.

To appreciate Waterloo's nineteenth-century domestic architecture, go left on Moore Street, left again on Fourth, left on South Main, and right on Third. At Market note the two nineteenth-century houses across the highway. Expansion of Illinois 3 will damage the appeal of the courthouse square and its surroundings in the near future.

If you are hungry turn left on Illinois 3 for the Lincoln Trail Restaurant just off the square at 108 North Market. To continue the tour, go south on Illinois 3 (Market) a short block, then right on Illinois 156. Follow Illinois 156 past a Victorian barn and the town library at 219 Park. A short distance beyond, turn left on Lakeview Drive, which becomes Maeystown Road. At four miles you see Wartburg, with its 1863 stone Lutheran church. Not quite two miles south another right at ill-marked KK — there's a red and white radio antenna on the right — will take you the mile and a half to Madonnaville, also endowed with fine stone buildings. Here the 1859 Church of the Immaculate Conception and a later rectory and school stand in a setting unmarred by asphalt or other assaults on its state of grace.

Backtrack to Maeystown Road and continue southeast to that German settlement, founded in 1852. Nearly all the village's buildings are on the National Register of Historic Places. But Maeystown's potent appeal has less to do with single buildings than with their intact relationship with one another, as well as the whole place's happy relationship to the hillside and the three creeks that meet here. Notice the large stone mill, the fine 1881 stone bridge and the many extant outbuildings. There is also a bed and breakfast inn above the general store, and a tavern and restaurant catercorner. Dominating the village is the 1860 Church of Christ; a stroll up Franklin will get you there. Maeystown's pines are reminiscent of Germany.

Continue two miles to Bluff Road, the old Kaskaskia Trail, where you turn left. The bluff-hugging road looks out onto an idyllic land, its rich farms now protected by dikes along the Mississippi. The neat houses occasionally have the distinctive one-story creole shape and gallery porches; you may also glimpse a log cabin or two.

Eight and a half miles southward — a couple of miles beyond Kidd Lake Road on the right and the Fults Hill Prairie Nature Preserve on the left — turn right on the presently unmarked Kaskaskia road; it goes straight over the railway, and just beyond is a house embellished with a number of lawn ornaments. Follow it to Stringtown Road, where you are obliged to turn left. This road leads to Fort de Chartres.

French grandeur has always had at least as much to do with French minds as with French economics or French military success. Unwilling to believe, even incapable of conceiving, that they were not in a position to emulate Spain's exploitation of American mineral wealth, the French convinced themselves that the Illinois country — including what is now Missouri — *had* to be rich in precious metals. That, and the vast deficits left by Louis XIV after his death in 1714, made them easy prey for the creative speculations of high-living gambler and financial wizard, John Law.

Louis XV's regent had met Scotsman Law at the gaming table. That acquaintance opened the way for Law. He eventually controlled most of France's taxes, revenue, and foreign trade — including the hoped-for riches of France's mines along the Mississippi. The first Fort de Chartres was built in 1720, partly for protection of the mines being developed across the river, partly for the missions along the river. Law's great power ended when the Mississippi Bubble, as his attempt to alchemize the French national debt into gold by way of junk bonds came to be called, popped. But his reorganization of the French empire in America, to which Fort de Chartres was essential, remained.

The original stone fort was completed in 1756 by royal engineer François Saucier, with rock quarried from the bluffs behind Prairie du Rocher, to the east. Replacing earlier versions in wood, it was to defend France's interests against hostile Indians and the rival British. The fort's design is in accord with seventeenth-century military architect Vauban's principles — bastions, sentry-boxes, moats, and ramparts.

Near the end of the stronghold's French life Pierre Laclede and Auguste Chouteau spent the winter here, just before founding St. Louis in 1764.

The British won Fort de Chartres in the French and Indian War. But they found the struggle with the encroaching Mississippi expensive and pointless; in 1770 General Gage, British commandant in America, declared the fort little better than a mere mark of possession. The British abandoned it soon afterward.

The walls, fifteen feet high and three thick, gradually

came down — helped a great deal by the departing British troops' crippling of the fort to keep it out of foreign hands. Reconstruction began after Illinois bought the site in 1913. But most of what you see now, including the impressive stone bastions, was built in the late 1980s, based on both archaeological evidence and British descriptions of the fort at the time of their occupation. Full reconstruction is impossible; the western wall and river gate are now under the levee separating the site from the river.

Behind the walls is Illinois' oldest datable building, a powder magazine built in 1756. In the absence of contemporary descriptions, the barracks here have been hypothetically outlined in timber, a technique known as "ghosting." A chapel, a museum, and an eighteenth-century-style shop are also within the walls.

Founded in 1722, the village of Prairie du Rocher stands where the prairie meets the bluffs — hence the name. It's three miles from Fort de Chartres, turning right as you exit on Illinois 155. The fort's stone was quarried from the great caverns visible to the left. After the creole-style village hall, turn right onto Market. The 1800 Creole House is on the left. A right at Duclos takes you to the Maison du Rocher, where they serve excellent homemade pies.

Creole French is still spoken by the older inhabitants of Prairie du Rocher. Pride in their heritage dates back two centuries; a traveler at the end of the eighteenth century observed that they had kept Americans at a distance by not selling them any of their land. "They knew that strangers, with customs and mores so different from theirs, would disrupt their precious tranquility, the peaceful harmony that they enjoyed."[4]

Follow Illinois 155 south through Modoc, continuing along the bluffs. In a few miles you cross the Kaskaskia

River. Turn right on Illinois 3 toward Ellis Grove. After about a quarter of a mile go right toward City Hall, where a left takes you through the town's faded shopping cluster. Beyond quilted-tin encased Wittenauer's, turn right at the stop sign.

After four miles of winding through the countryside and paralleling the railroad south, you arrive at the pristine white Pierre Menard house. Built in 1800 in the style of a minor Louisiana plantation, it is one of the prettiest dwellings in the St. Louis region.

French Canadian Menard was a successful business-man and a partner of Ste Genevieve's Felix Vallé. In 1818 he was elected Illinois' first lieutenant governor, but only after a state constitutional amendment made an allowance for his foreign birth.

The famously hospitable Menard house is a monu-ment to creole domesticity. The exterior, graceful and stately without being pretentious, is matched by a welcoming and finely detailed interior. The ground floor offers a slide show and a collection of artifacts, including the slippers in which Menard's daughter Alzira danced with the Marquis de Lafayette in 1825. A walk around the herb garden, the kitchen, the smokehouse and the spring house completes the visit.

A left just beyond the house leads you to Fort Kaskaskia State Historic Site. Atop the bluff appear the earthworks of the fort.

When the British won the French and Indian War, Kaskaskia's French inhabitants destroyed the palisade stronghold rather than let the British make use of it.

This hostility toward the British — who had driven Nova Scotia's Acadians off their lands a short time before — was so widespread in French Illinois that a great number of creoles chose to migrate across the river to places like Ste Genevieve rather than submit to the rule of their hereditary enemy.

Anti-British feeling no doubt explains why Kaskaskia fell to George Rogers Clark and his Kentucky "Long Knives" without a shot in July, 1778. Cahokia, as well as the British stronghold at Vincennes, Indiana, fell shortly thereafter. Clark's bold plan to capture Britain's northwest possessions for the new republic succeeded.

After the Revolution Kaskaskia's inhabitants perhaps regretted their welcome of the Americans. Anarchy overwhelmed the town as John Dodge of Connecticut and his desperados refortified this site, terrorizing the populace for two years in the 1780s.

It was another enemy who was to destroy Kaskaskia, however. Drive farther along the bluff to the scenic overlook of the Kaskaskia River's confluence with the Mississippi. Below you is the watery site of the old creole town, which was founded in 1703 and in time became so prosperous that it was chosen as the first capital of Illinois. In 1881 the monstrously engorged Mississippi charged eastward into the Kaskaskia River's channel, engulfing part of the city. As one writer described it, "The sky and the turbid Mississippi" met and became one. "There were waters over the heavens and waters under the heavens. A wall like a moving dam swept across the world and filled it."[5] Subsequent spring floods continued the damage and by 1913 Kaskaskia had completely disappeared. Its cemeteries were moved just south of the overlook, while the bell Louis XV had given its church was relocated across the new path of the Mississippi.

Head back to the river road and turn left. A few miles south Pierre Menard's name has been attached to architecture more somber than his plantation-style house. The Menard State Correctional Institution, built of gold stone in grand eighteenth-century French style, has some curious iconography. The relief in the pediment combines a padlock with crossed keys, Moses' tablets and the scales of Justice. All are displayed against a brilliant sun. At the entrance, between two Romanesque lions, is a tree whose limbs have been lopped off and whose bark is peeled back to reveal a text which is now illegible.

You might ponder this as you return to St. Louis, which you may do one of two ways. Time and weather encouraging, backtrack to Fort Kaskaskia and follow the Shawneetown Trail to Illinois 3. Take Illinois 3 north to Ellis Grove, just beyond which a well-marked left will take you back to Modoc and Prairie du Rocher. Go right on Illinois 155 at Prairie du Rocher, then quickly left toward Fults. At a T with Maeystown Road, a left will keep you on Bluff Road which now clings less closely to the bluff. This takes you to Valmeyer. Turn left at the stop sign and then right on Lake Street; it's the second street after the railroad tracks. Lake Street turns into Bluff Road. There is a T intersection near the invisible town of Fountain. Turn right and then left at the foot of the bluff. You join Illinois 3 above Columbia.

For a prairie experience, backtrack to Fort Kaskaskia State Historic Site and follow the Shawneetown Trail to Illinois 3; head north and you will pass by Ellis Grove and Evansville and through Red Bud.

For information call:
Church of the Holy Family 618-332-1782
Fort de Chartres 618-284-7230
Fort Kaskaskia State Historic Site 618-859-3741
Fults Hill Prairie Nature Preserve 618-826-2706
Jarrot House 618-332-1782
Monroe County Courthouse 618-332-1782
Pierre Menard Home 618-859-3031
Sts. Peter and Paul 618-939-6426

Bolduc House, Ste Genevieve

Begins at exit 154, Interstate 55

The phrase "frontier life" conjures up images of grizzly bears and grizzly men, a life of rough and ready aggression. But Missouri's first frontier was French, and the French enjoyed gentle relations with the land and with one another. Ste Genevieve, Missouri's oldest town, is still a lesson in that charming and least disruptive of cultures. The grace of its faded exoticism makes even a brief visit there highly rewarding.

Take I-55 to exit 154 and turn right (south) on U.S. Highway 61. The number of lawn madonnas here tells you that this is Catholic country. After about six and a half miles the rolling landscape breaks, revealing the vast, almost magically white Mississippi Lime works, largest in the United States. Ste Genevieve's underpinning is a massive limestone formation 98.5 percent pure calcium.

Just beyond, at the brown Felix Vallé State Historical Site arrow, turn left on Market Street. The town's creole nonchalance appears immediately: note the casual way many of the eighteenth- and nineteenth-century houses sit on their lots and the imprecise nature of the street grid. Tiny curved Boyer Place is an example. At 807 Market stands the 1787 François Bernier House, one of the dozens that make Ste Genevieve richer in eighteenth-century creole buildings than any other place on the continent.

Farther down Market, the massive Knights of Columbus house on the right, and, on the left across Fourth, the church, school, and convent complex, again demonstrate Catholicism's vigor in this area.

On the right at Market and Second an 1869 red brick Lutheran church is a reminder of the important German immigration here. Beyond appears the back of the Bolduc House, which we will visit shortly. Its distinctive broken-pitch roofs and its wood, plaster and stone walls let you know that you're in a foreign place.

Stop first for a visit to the Great River Road Interpretive Center, just across Main. Built of cedar, like many of Ste Genevieve's creole homes, the center offers exhibitions and a video about the town.

As the video suggests, the founding date of Ste Genevieve is problematic. Enthusiasts used to say that the town was established in 1725. Local historians have so long declared 1735 as founding year that the city celebrated its 250th anniversary in 1985. But Carl Ekberg, in his excellent *Colonial Ste Genevieve*, places birth date at about 1750, or perhaps a few years earlier.

In any event, the town founded whenever it was is not the town we see today, but another located three miles downstream. In June of 1785, *l'année des grands eaux*, a flood rose to the rooftops of that Ste Genevieve, prompting a move to the present higher ground.

There has also been confusion about why the town was founded. The traditional explanation, that the town originated as a lead depot, has given way to the idea that it was the fertile Grand Champs which attracted farmers from Kaskaskia, across the river, then others from Canada, France, and the French Caribbean.

Now go south on Main to the Bolduc House. In this beautifully restored structure we have the quintessential creole blend of Old World and New. Its palisade fence is reminiscent of Indian stockades like the ones at Cahokia Mounds. The roof line derives from Norman and/or

Mayan antecedents. The gallery porch follows Caribbean practice.

The last of the once wealthy Bolducs to live here, an aged spinster, left in the late 1940s. The Colonial Dames then restored the house, finding many of the family pieces now on display.

The tour begins in the *salle*, an all-purpose living area. It is reasonable to suppose (and owners of old Ste Genevieve houses invariably do) that materials from Old Town structures were salvaged for their post-1785 analogues, a claim made for the Bolduc salle. The water-stained armoire likewise seems to have survived the inundation. Madame Bolduc's glasses sit on the dining table. To the left of the fireplace hangs a rococo bread safe whose key Madame kept in her apron.

The bedroom's old spread and curtains were found in the attic. The crucifix here shows a thick-set Christ patterned on the short and stocky locals.

Through the foyer, used as Monsieur Bolduc's office, you exit onto the rear porch. The river valley climate, as hot in summer as the Caribbean's, made porches desirable. Waterproofing them was a lesser consideration than that of the house proper, which explains why their roof pitch is not as steep. Note the wood farm tools against the wall.

In 1815 the Bolducs enclosed a corner of this porch for a kitchen. Within, an unstuccoed wall reveals creole vertical-log construction, the fourth log from each corner slanting inward for stability.

The bowl carved from a tree stump here was a gift from the Indians. Notice the kettle hook in the fireplace, the coffee bean roaster and the waffle iron. Atop the hutch near the doorway is a spherical wire gadget, an eighteenth-century salad dryer. Attractive and functional, these tools connote a way of life that was anything but primitive. In fact, life in colonial Ste Genevieve compared favorably with that in the French provinces.

Kitchens like this produced multi-course menus combining French food sense with American ingredients. Soup, fish, sausage and pork, fruits, cheeses, and tarts were all washed down with French or Spanish wines, local beer and cider.

Creole palates did not accept all indigenous products. Corn was for animals and tomatoes were poisonous. But catfish was considered "very good and delicate," especially when fried in bear oil — which was also used in salads. Though bear oil has fallen from favor, another Ste Genevieve staple appears on tables today: watermelon. What is to us the most ordinary of fruits was a great delicacy for the French:

> . . . in eating them it seems as if you have a sponge soaked in Alicante wine dissolving in your mouth, for the juice is crimson and exquisitely flavored. . . . You pick these melons in the morning before sunrise and place them in the shade. In this fashion they maintain perfectly their freshness, which they then transmit to those who eat them.[1]

The everyday dress of the people around the table was more American than the menu. Even gentlemen bound their pigtails with eelskin, and wore checked shirts and jeans-like pantaloons. Both sexes wore moccasins. On Sundays, however, silver buckled shoes replaced the moccasins, knee britches and silk stockings the men's dungarees, and ruffled linen the checked shirts. Ladies likewise doffed calico and gingham to don fur-trimmed silk taffetas.

Ste Genevieve's sartorial mix was matched by its ethnic makeup. French, Indians and blacks were blended in a manner unthinkable in the old country, or, for that matter, in most places in the new. Townsman Charles Aimé's household, to name one of many examples, included his

Osage Indian wife, six mestizo children and a retired blind slave named Nago.[2]

Aimé's marriage was far from unusual — and anything but scandalous. Pierre Viriat of nearby Mine La Motte purchased a mulatto slave named Rodde Christi, freed her and then married her in May 1801, with the best of Ste Genevieve society as witnesses.[3]

Mixing was the Ste Genevieve way. Even household gardens mingled savory and medicinal herbs with flowers, vegetables, shrubs and fruit trees. Local fruits, especially apples, were praised up and down the river.

Walk through the side gate of the Bolduc House's garden to the 1820s Bolduc-Le Meilleur House, which has a creole appearance. Its timber and nogging structure, however, is purely American. The interior may be visited furnishings are of the period but not of the family.

Across Market is the 1785 Jean-Baptiste Vallé House, whose stuccoed vertical logs rest on a sill of forty-six-foot oak beams.

As its interracial marriages may suggest, Ste Genevieve did not have a rigid social structure. But it did have a power elite. The Vallés dominated the town from the early 1760s when François Vallé controlled affairs under the French and then under the Spanish; after the Louisiana Purchase, the Americans appointed his son Jean-Baptiste civil commandant. The Vallé house, not open to the public, even now emanates an atmosphere of power. What is purported to be the oldest rose garden west of the Mississippi can be seen through the gate at 99 South Main.

Continue up Main. A white picket fence marks the Vital St. Gemme Beauvais house. This acorn-topped enclosure is historically incorrect. Eighteenth-century Ste Genevieve had a passion for pickets, contemporary sources relate, but their pickets were in fact palisades. Those of the Vital St. Gemme Beauvais house were eight to ten inches in diameter. We know this fact thanks to a boarder here, Henry Brackenridge of Pittsburgh. Young Brackenridge's father wanted him to learn French. He didn't have to ship his progeny to Paris: France was on the Mississippi, too. Brackenridge explained that the palisades served more against animals than enemies. Livestock in relaxed Ste Genevieve style foraged where it would.

Backtrack north on Main Street past the 1848 white-columned St. Gemme Beauvais Inn at Jefferson. Like the Bolduc-Le Meilleur House, it is a sign of changing times: both the appearance and construction are American. A left on Washington takes you past an L-shaped red brick house on the right and, on the left, the town's first public school, built in 1859. As you turn left onto Second note the near-twin houses.

Continue on Second to Merchant. On the southeast corner sits the Felix Vallé House, open to the public. It was built in 1818 by a Polish Jew from Philadelphia in that city's Federal style. Jean-Baptiste Vallé bought it in 1824 as headquarters for his vast commercial interests, some of which were shared with Pierre Menard. Around 1835 Jean-Baptiste's fourth son, Felix, took up residence here. Felix, like the house, reflects the Americanization of Ste Genevieve: a Kentucky education made him fluent in both French and English. He used the building as both business headquarters and residence.

The Vallés' enterprises included trade with the Indians. Much has been made of the ease of Franco-Indian relations. French frontiersmen, both trappers and missionaries, had long accepted the Indians both as companions and converts. This amity, which contrasts with Anglo-Indian friction, is also a reflection of different economic interests. French fur merchants profited from Indian expertise; Anglo-American farmers needed Indian lands but not the Indians themselves.

French interracial ease was not limited to commerce, as the Aimé and Viriat households show. Brackenridge said the boys of Ste Genevieve practiced shooting bow and arrow with their Indian peers, and another observer saw creole children playing pell-mell with Peoria Indians in the town's dusty streets.

Intimacy between the races took on a ceremonial aspect on New Year's Day. Christian Schultz, a nineteenth-century visitor, noticed that individuals of all races and stations kissed on January 1: "The negro kisses his mistress, the master kisses his wenches . . . as a token of reconciliation, and forgetfulness of all past animosities." Later that day, as he was shaving, he himself was surrounded by Peoria Indians — eight of them — who "kissed me so completely that I had not an atom of lather remaining on my face."[4]

As these New Year's kisses would suggest, relations between Ste Genevieve's creoles and their black servants were also gentler than in the Anglo-American colonies. The outbuildings at the rear of the Felix Vallé House are thought to have been slave quarters. Slaveholding in colonial Ste Genevieve was regulated by the relatively humane *Code Noir* elaborated under Louis XIV's minister, Colbert. One of its fifty-five articles gave slaves the right to take their masters to court for violations of the code. Another provided for free weekends when they might hire themselves out and pocket the proceeds. One example of the prevalent good will is Felix Vallé's legacy of $300 each — a considerable sum in 1877 — to former slaves Basile, Zabette and Madeleine.

West on Merchant Street sits a cluster of historic houses. One of them, the 1827 Linn House, was home of the Missouri senator instrumental in the U.S. acquisition of Oregon. Downtown begins here, with its restaurants and shops and the glorious Orris, once a cinema, now a restaurant and night club. Cross Third Street and park in front of the town museum.

To the left on Third is a granite reminder of El Camino Real. The King's Highway was built from here to St. Louis in 1779 so that the latter town might send aid to Ste Genevieve. Things worked out otherwise. In 1780 Ste Genevieve's sixty-man militia went to St. Louis, valiantly helping repel a fierce Anglo-Indian attack.

Across the street is the Anvil Restaurant, with its own commentary on the pervasive presence of the past in Ste Genevieve: among the old photographs on the wall a plaque announces, "In 1827 Nothing Happened Here." The Anvil's liver dumplings are memorable, however.

This restaurant is one of several stops on the *guignolée,* a traditional creole New Year's Eve celebration which takes costumed men door to door, singing an ancient request for donations for Twelfth Night festivities. The creole equivalent of trick or treat, the song offered the head of each household a choice: a glass of wine or a dance with available daughters.

Ste Genevieve's museum is an old-fashioned *Wunderkammer* full of quirky mementoes. A case of Audubon's stuffed birds sits atop a safe Jesse James robbed; a six-legged frog floats in a jar across the room from Pius XII's white zucchetto.

Other displays help in understanding Ste Genevieve. There are two evaporating vessels used to make salt at nearby La Saline Creek. Ten gallons of the creek's water yielded about three pounds of salt; four were necessary to salt a twenty-pound ham. Opposite is a rough wooden trough used in that process, essential to early Ste Genevieve's export trade. Activity at La Saline ended in 1825 when steamboats made shipment of salt from the Gulf of Mexico more economical.

The big neo-Gothic church across DuBourg Place is

more important as a symbol than as architecture. Though built in 1888, when the local population was no longer French-dominated, it has much that is French about it, including a statue of the patron saint of France, Joan of Arc, who is asked, *Priez pour nous*. The architect was an Alsatian priest; Odile Vallé, Felix's wife, defrayed two-thirds of the building expense. Note the French, German and English names on the stained glass windows and the linoleum *intarsio* floors. The last chapel on the left contains several Vallé tombstones.

At the corner of Merchant and Fourth sits the 1784 Maison Guibourd-Vallé. Inside, the beaded beams, low inner doorways and "Christian" outer doors, so named because their panels form a cross over an open Bible, are fine examples of creole woodwork. A visit to the attic affords the best look at creole construction techniques; the triangular geometry of Norman trusses and beams, punctuated by the wooden pegs which hold all together, is worth the tour.

The house was owned by Jules Felix Vallé, direct descendant of the last Vallé commandant of Ste Genevieve, until 1949, when it passed to his wife, a St. Louisan whose youth had been spent on the stage. She didn't care for the dark simplicity of the house's creole furniture and replaced it with the ebullient chinoiserie you see there now. An Indian prince, who lived in the guesthouse, accompanied Mrs. Vallé around Ste Genevieve in his Rolls Royce.

Return to your car and take Merchant to Fifth. Across Fifth, in Memorial Cemetery, Felix and Odile Vallé and others rest under elevated New Orleans-style stones, a necessity in that swampy city but here simply a matter of fashion. The bodies are in graves below.

Left on Fifth to Market and then left again. Across DuBourg Place stands the county courthouse, unidentified by any sign. Could this be a latter-day reflection of the peaceable nature of the creoles, who rarely needed courts? Across Third Street is the Price Building, oldest brick structure west of the Mississippi. Its date shifts mysteriously according to the source you consult: 1785, 1795, 1800, or 1804.

Right onto Third Street past the Southern Hotel, built, like the Felix Vallé House, in the Federal style. A left on South Gabouri takes you past what remains of the 1784 François Vallé II House. He, like his father and younger brother, served as commandant of Ste Genevieve.

At Main look across the street to the decrepit 1795 Moses Austin House, atop a slight hillock. To the left of it is an equally decayed house in a garden of ghost cars.

Cross the bridge and veer left; Main becomes St. Mary's Road south of Gabouri Creek. On the right appears the Green Tree Inn, built almost completely of walnut in 1790 by François Janis. In 1804 he turned it into an inn to accommodate American travelers.

Continue south past the Amoureaux House, one of three surviving *poteaux-en-terre* (vertical posts directly in the earth) structures. A few yards farther down, also on the right, is another such structure, the Bequette-Ribault House.

At the intersection of St. Mary's Road and U.S. 61, head south (left) for one and a half miles. Just after the Ste Genevieve Jaycees Sports Complex, you will see two dark red sheds on the right. Beyond them, turn into the driveway of a crumbling clapboarded vertical-log house. Local tradition has it — incorrectly — that this was the home of Pierre Charles de Hault, Seigneur de Lassus, de St. Vrain, and de Luzières, Chevalier de Grand Croix de l'Ordre Royal de St. Michel, Civil and Military Commandant of New Bourbon.

This nobleman, fleeing the French revolution, had grand yet not foolish hopes for a new society here. But river

valley fevers laid him low, their diminished situation un-
balanced his wife, and his utopian plans bore meager fruit.
De Lassus died a disappointed man in 1806. New Bourbon,
the town he founded atop this bluff, did not long survive
him. Materials from his house there were probably used in
the structure before you.

Turn around and look across the road — this is the
Grand Champs, the "Big Field." Basis of early Ste
Genevieve's economy, the field's 7,000 acres were divided
into narrow strips running between the river and the bluffs.
It was worked this way until 1907.

The creole farmers fenced it all to keep animals out.
Anyone whose fence section failed in this purpose was
responsible for damages. After sowing their crops farmers
shut the gates; anyone entering the Grand Champs before
harvest faced stiff penalties. "It was up to God and the
Mississippi to determine how the crop would fare . . ."[5]
The crop often did well; Ste Genevieve, despite its nickname Misère, was the breadbasket of Upper Louisiana.
Nature's abundance had much to do with the easy life here.

The hummock you see in the middle of the field is an
Indian mound.

Turn right (south) on U.S. 61. The beautiful bluff road
will take you to St. Mary's, a scruffy place crowned by a
pretty brick church. In the center of town a sign directs you
left to Kaskaskia Bell State Park. Cross the shallow trickle —
which was the Mississippi until an 1881 flood pushed that
river into the bed of the Kaskaskia. State boundaries remained as originally drawn; even though you are still west
of the Mississippi, you are in Illinois.

Signs for the Kaskaskia Bell direct you across a
floodplain. It is almost entirely cultivated, but civilization
has left few other traces here. The present fragility of this
isolated tract belies a surprisingly solid history.

As an expanding village of missionaries, Indians, *coureurs des bois,* and farmers, Old Kaskaskia was important enough to merit the attention of Louis XV. In 1741 the Bourbon monarch even sent the community a gift. The bell giving the site its name now hangs in a brick shelter next to the late nineteenth-century church. Its inscription reads: *POUR LEGLISE DES ILLINOIS PAR LES SOINS DU ROI DOUTRE LEAU* — "for the church of the Illinois as a gift of the king across the sea."

Kaskaskia grew so much, in fact, that its inhabitants' later search for farmland led them across the river to Ste Genevieve's Grand Champs: it was enterprising Kaskaskians who founded Missouri's oldest town. Later, Kaskaskian creoles fleeing the unsympathetic English, or the lawless Americans, found refuge in Ste Genevieve's familiar Frenchness.

A man who knew Ste Genevieve well was serving as Kaskaskia's commandant at the outbreak of the American Revolution. Philippe de Rocheblave had tried to bolster anti-American efforts in Spanish Louisiana by predicting that American victory would make it impossible for any European nation to maintain colonies in North America. His attempts were for naught, but the history of the next three-quarters of a century proved how correct he was.

At the time of George Rogers Clark's swift occupation of Kaskaskia, his men apprehended de Rocheblave in his nightshirt. As a signal of American victory, they rang Louis XV's bell, earning it the sobriquet of "The Liberty Bell of the West."

Take U.S. 61 north to Ste Genevieve and I-55.

For information call:
Bequette-Ribault House 1-883-7171
Bolduc House 1-883-3105
Bolduc-Le Meilleur House 1-883-3105
Felix Vallé State Historic Site (house) 1-883-7102
Great River Road Interpretive Center 1-883-7097
Maison Guibourd-Vallé 1-883-7544
Ste Genevieve Museum 1-883-3461

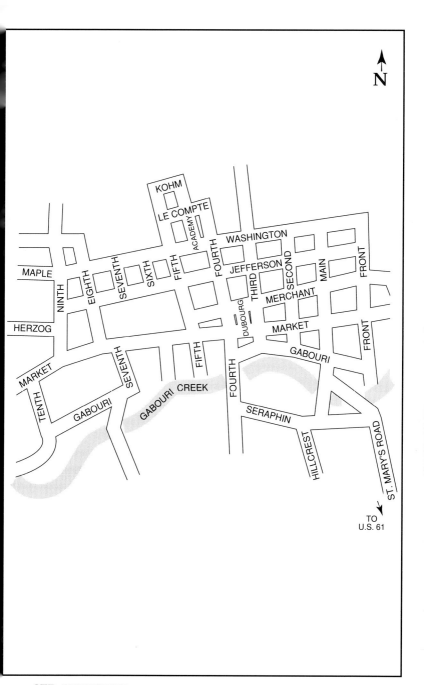

STE GENEVIEVE

Barn, Altenburg

The Varieties of Religious Experience   3

Begins at exit 105 on Interstate 55, 92.5 miles south
of Interstate 70

French missionaries' zeal often produced a grand effect on
the Indians in early America. Less responsive, paradoxi-
cally, were the missionaries' Creole cousins, whose levity
in religious matters was notorious.

After the Louisiana Purchase ended Catholicism's
monopoly here, new settlers brought Missouri different
religions, and Catholicism itself underwent a revival.
Methodist, Lutheran, and Catholic efforts have left a kind
of moral mosaic on the landscape. This itinerary links
places where each group made its distinctive mark during
the first decades of the nineteenth century.

Attractions in Perry and Cape Girardeau counties are
not exclusively religious, however. Despite some recent
roadside sprawl, the land itself is interesting. Especially
beautiful is the park set aside to commemorate a tragic
episode in Cherokee history, the Trail of Tears State Park.
The first stop also has no religious connotation, only the
irresistible appeal of old mills and covered bridges.

After leaving I-55, follow U.S. 61 west to Jackson. The
Cape Girardeau County courthouse dominates the view
after you enter town. If you're hungry, the Rainbow
Restaurant at 127 South High, off the courthouse square,
offers plain old-fashioned fare.

Continue on U.S. 61 through Jackson to its junction with
Missouri 34/72. Turn right. Veer left onto Missouri 34 at
the brown Bollinger Mill sign three and a half miles west

of U.S. 61. About five miles beyond, a left on OO (then straight on HH) takes you into Burfordville, where you will find the picturesque mill and its neighboring covered bridge. Cross this span, completed as a toll bridge in 1868, for a view of the mill complex. The dam, and the stone portion of the mill, date from 1825. The brick-upper section replaced a frame antecedent burnt by Union soldiers in the Civil War because of its owners' Confederate leanings.

The mill exerts the ancient fascination both of artfully channeled water and of the complex milling process. Its half-submerged lower chamber has a downright medieval atmosphere. The mill, which functioned commercially through 1950, still grinds meal; a demonstration is part of the tour.

To go back to Missouri 34, take the gravel fork to the right, which parallels Burfordville's main street. Here you can see more of the hamlet's fine collection of gingerbread porches.

Follow Missouri 34 back to U.S. 61, which you take south, away from Jackson. Turn left at the first stoplight — Shawnee Avenue — then quickly right onto Old Cape Road. Turn left soon after on Bainbridge where you will see an Old McKendree Chapel sign. Continue almost two miles to an historical marker. Turn left, noting an elegant two-story dogtrot cabin on the right. At the end of this lane is Old McKendree Chapel.

The log structure, first Methodist Church west of the Mississippi, is reverently protected by a metal canopy. Its white-washed simplicity suggests the plainness of pioneer life. Nonetheless, when it was built in 1819, Methodists considered it the finest meeting house in all the western country.

Ministers of any cult faced a great challenge on the frontier. The pioneers, independent individuals by definition, were not inclined to think much about any power beyond themselves. Yet they did have unspoken longings that not even felling the great forest could satisfy. Wilderness revivals and camp meetings were a way of reaching frontiersmen.

These religious gatherings provided high drama and low

comedy as well. Attendants were often seized by "the jerks." One man, to describe the feeling of the Holy Spirit that had come over him during a revival, jumped about exclaiming, "Slick as a peeled onion! Slick as a peeled onion!" A pastor who preached revivals here was called "Rough and Ready Watts," for being as handy with his fists as with his Bible. He boasted of his converts as "scalps he had taken for the Lord."[1]

The solitude of the wilderness, deepened by the American habit of living on isolated farms, took a toll especially on the women. Camp meetings' virtuous goals justified what was for many the sole occasion of social intercourse.

McKendree's site, first used for Methodist meetings in 1806, was ideal for the workings of both the Spirit and the picnic. It was chosen because its slight elevation caught the breezes, its fine oaks and maples provided shade, and its sweet-water spring gave refreshment.

The chapel, built of very large hand-hewn poplar logs, has a simple plastered interior. One epithet for the elaborate traditional faith frontiersmen rejected was "high steeple religion." McKendree is the opposite of that.

Go back to U.S. 61 and turn right. At the intersection of U.S. 61 and Missouri 34/72 note the St. Louis Iron Mountain and Southern steam engine, which puffs south on Saturdays and Sundays. A ticket buys visitors a ten-mile trip through the surrounding countryside on the only operating steam train in Missouri. A supper journey is offered on Saturday nights. The engine is a 1946 H.K. Porter; the cars and caboose date from the 1920s.

Continue on U.S. 61 back through Jackson. A distance beyond the city limits turn right on Y to Oriole. This is a lush valley with several beautiful farmhouses. After seven and a half miles, turn right onto V and cross the bridge.

Three miles beyond turn left onto Missouri 177 and then quickly right into the Trail of Tears State Park, so named for an American tragedy, the shameful forced migration of Cherokees from their lands in the east to Oklahoma.

The interpretive center, to the left just after the entrance, houses first-rate exhibits on the park's nature and history. Displays tell, for instance, about Sequoyah's invention of a Cherokee syllabary in 1821. Thousands of Cherokees, mostly town dwellers, soon learned to read and write. The tribe enjoyed a cultural revival in the 1820s with the establishment of schools, a newspaper, and a museum. But Cherokee literacy could do nothing against their white neighbors' greed. After gold was discovered on their territory they were corralled into disease-ridden camps and marched west in 1838-39.

One out of four Cherokees succumbed on the way, including Princess Otahki, the daughter of an ordained Baptist preacher, Chief Jesse Bushyhead. There is a monument to her nearby.

A map of the park, available at the interpretive center, will help you proceed to the park's overlook high above the Mississippi. A plaque commemorates Father Marquette's trip down this river in 1673.

Exit the park. Turn right on Missouri 177 which you follow to U.S. 61. Turn right and drive a mile and a half north through Fruitland. Turn right on C for Pocahontas. At C and Pocahontas' Main Street you see, a block to the left and a block to the right, the town's two red brick Lutheran churches. Note the ex-grocery store on the corner.

Follow C several miles north. After Tric's Family Restaurant turn right onto A where a sign proclaims "Stadt Altenburg, DDR 976, US 1839." Behind this straightforward emblem of traditionalism lies a story of high melodrama and real heroism.

It begins in early-nineteenth-century Germany. A band of Saxons, fearful of the softening of their state church's Lutheranism, decided to come to the New World where they might practice their old faith free of government harassment.

They had a charismatic leader, Martin Stephan. His morals, unfortunately, were nowhere near so pure as his followers' faith. Even before leaving Germany, Stephan had been brought to trial on charges of seducing a girl. The emigrants dismissed the case as calumny. They likewise overlooked Stephan's tendency toward extravagance in matters of money and temperament. During their Atlantic passage, for instance, he himself indulged in bouts of rage but branded his ill-fed third-class passengers sinners when they made dumplings to supplement their Sunday dinner. In spite of his erratic behavior they elected him bishop, even signing pledges of submission upon arrival in St. Louis.

The 600 Lutherans' confidence in their autocratic leader must have faltered a little at his next decision. He bought over 4,400 acres of uncleared, infertile land in this isolated spot. Only a small percentage of his group were farmers. The overwhelming majority — craftsmen, professionals, and merchants — had talents much in demand in thriving St. Louis, but hardly suited for conquering the wilderness. Stephan's few farmers could not work miracles; the Saxons would have starved the first winter had not the Presbyterians of nearby Brazeau given them food.

Stephan's hold on his followers was not broken, however, until a couple of girls he had seduced after his arrival in America spoke out. The Saxons now turned on the man they had considered their "Noah, Moses and Israel." They ferried him across the river and deposited him on the Illinois shore. His housemaid Louise, the pastor's confessed mistress, later joined him in exile.

The first of Altenburg's two Lutheran churches appears on the right soon after the town sign. A number of picturesque cottages follow. Don't overlook the stores which make Altenburg's a true downtown.

On the right, an 1839 Saxon log house stands under a shelter in the town's "Mini Central Park." Just beyond is the first home of Concordia Seminary, founded here in 1839 and moved to St. Louis ten years later. Its original seven male students, joined shortly by girls, were taught Latin, Greek, Hebrew, German, French, and English — as well as religion and the arts and sciences.

This ambitious curriculum reflected a society vigorous in spite of Stephan's malfeasance. With the help of a forceful and eloquent pastor, C.F.W. Walther, the Saxons' improbable Perry County experiment produced not only Concordia Seminary, but also, in time, the Lutheran Church — Missouri Synod.

A few yards beyond turn right to the 1867 Trinity Lutheran Church. Next door is the original 1845 edifice, later a school, now a museum.

Back on A, turn right toward the Mississippi. At the foot of the bluff, make a right onto gravel Tower Rock Road (County Road 460) for the nature area set aside by President Grant in 1871. It's a potholed mile and a half to the geological peculiarity where French missionaries planted a cross in 1699. On the way note the magnificent inverted thunderbird-like steel structures of a suspended gas line on its way from Texas to Chicago. The Rock and its surroundings are as rough as the road.

Backtrack to A and turn right for Wittenberg, site of the Saxons' arrival in Perry County and of Stephan's chilly send-off. It may not look like much now, but Wittenberg, the first of the five towns the Saxons founded, was once the economic hub of Perry County. In steamboat days farmers shipped livestock upriver from here. Incoming cargo for the town's two waterfront stores was unloaded to cries of "Bumblebee" and "Firefly," the stevedores' way of sending goods to the right place.

The railroad era brought more stores, a hotel, livery

stables, and a bank. But in 1907 a fire destroyed much of the town and severe flooding in 1941-2 finished off most of what remained.

A right onto the gravel road will take you past a run-down gallery-porched house and the post office, over the railroad tracks, and left past a stone smokestack, last fragment of a flour mill. Continue a few yards to a T intersection — all mud and gravel — and turn right for the stone marker commemorating the Saxons' landing. An evangelical verse proclaims, "Christ must increase but I must decrease." Wittenberg has.

Backtrack to Altenburg. Continue straight on A and C which lead quickly to Frohna's notable collection of storefronts. Follow C as it turns right opposite the post office. As you proceed down the slope, note on the left the 1874 Concordia Lutheran Church and the 1898 brick school. At the bottom, turn right on Saxon Memorial Drive. The old farmstead at the top of the hill is open to the public. Built in 1820 by a slaveholding Southerner, it was sold in 1842 to a Saxon family who owned it until 1957. The complex is interesting, especially the slave cabins and an unusual barn chock-full of nineteenth-century agricultural tools.

Return to C and turn right for Brazeau, the Presbyterian settlement which helped the Saxons through their first winter. Immediately after the town sign turn right into the parking lot of the 1852 church. Its double doors kept the sexes apart as did those of the much later Parish Hall. Back on C note the Gothic cottage opposite the Post Office.

Follow C two miles out of Brazeau, where a left onto D leads you back to 61. Head north (right) toward Perryville. You'll pass through Longtown, with its quaint houses and a 1912 brick Lutheran church. As you approach Perryville look to the left for the low-steepled 1914 Methodist York Chapel.

Follow U.S. 61 through Perryville and turn left on

Missouri 51. A right on T brings you to St. Mary of the Barrens, whose name reflects the surrounding area's relative lack of trees, a surprise in heavily forested southeastern Missouri. The complex, high-steeple religion at its most elaborate, also comes as a surprise. But St. Mary's was born under an enthusiastic star, and has always stood out impressively against the countryside around it.

The Catholic settlers who arrived here from Kentucky in 1801 brought a religious fervor equal to that of the Saxons. But unlike the Saxons, no pastor accompanied them; they had to look to themselves for religious observance. On Sundays they met once to recite the mass, again to say the rosary and sing hymns, and a third time to offer catechism to children and adults. Father Dunand of Florissant, who began to visit a few years after their arrival here, was impressed:

> I imagined myself carried back to the blessed epoch of the birth of the Church. I fancied I saw those first Christians instructed by the Apostles and so united that they were but one heart and soul. [2]

When Bishop William DuBourg chose St. Louis as the seat of his diocese, Dunand suggested that DuBourg might found a seminary in the Barrens. Shortly after the new bishop's arrival in St. Louis, the settlers offered 640 acres and a building for this purpose. DuBourg accepted and work on a seminary, one of the first four in the United States, began quickly.

The bishop sent a group of Vincentians headed by Father Joseph Rosati to help. The sturdy Rosati, a Neapolitan, could often be found sweating with the locals at the construction site. This roll-up-the-sleeves approach helped acquaint Rosati with the settlers, whom he described to a colleague as "the finest people in the world, anxious to hear the word of God, to frequent the sacraments and to lead a simple life." [3]

"... Absolutely devoid of self-seeking," Rosati himself was as lovable as he was competent. His Vincentian superior, Felix de Andreis, added that "All who know him are fascinated by the piety and cheerful geniality of his conversation. I have not the slightest doubt that before long they will want to make him bishop."[4]

The prediction proved accurate. Rosati's duties expanded rapidly; he was named pastor of the Barrens, superior of the religious community there, professor in the seminary, and, after Felix de Andreis' death in 1820, director of novices and superior of the Vincentians in America. In 1822 Rome named him Bishop of Tenagra and Vicar Apostolic of the Territories of Mississippi and Alabama.

Rosati protested: the appointment would take him away from his much-loved Barrens. Rome compromised. He was to be coadjutor to Bishop DuBourg. In March 1824 he became the first bishop consecrated west of the Mississippi, but continued on at St. Mary's. When Rome tried to move him to New Orleans, he again declared that he wanted to stay in Missouri, "where I would prefer to eat corn bread and to be poor the rest of my life than to have all my comforts in Louisiana."[5]

Rosati's affection bore fruit. The Vincentians in Rome trained a Neapolitan monk in stone cutting and sent him to the Barrens with plans for a Baroque stone church. The pope sent 631 scudi to start construction. Rosati laid the cornerstone on January 1, 1827, placing in it papal, Napoleonic, and American coins. A former student of Rosati's, the Flemish Father DeNeckere, obtained from the Baroness of Gesegham a wealth of ceremonial robes, an organ and a printing press for the new church.

The church, completed in 1837, got a new facade in 1913. The interior, remodeled in the late-nineteenth century and touched up in the twentieth, is also quite different from the original. But despite its slightly goofy rendering of

Renaissance and baroque art, it does have an Italian air.

A 1930 chapel sits off the right aisle. The Madonna's 1830 apparitions to St. Catherine Labouré in Paris are shown in stained glass and mural decoration. This event engendered the devotion to the Miraculous Medal, facsimiles of which are available here.

A chamber with 60,000 votive lights opens to the right of the Miraculous Medal altar. Romantics might expect a room brilliant with candles, but technology has reached the Barrens: the votive "flames" are stacked trays of diodes, glowing yellow green.

Vincentian leader Felix de Andreis' tomb is to the right of the medal chapel. He has been nominated for sainthood.

This tour's landscapes have each had a kind of fitness for the religious efforts they have witnessed. It was right that the hymn-singing, soul-saving, camp-meeting Methodists build their first Missouri church on a breezy hillock in a great grove of oaks. It was right that the Saxon Lutherans test their dour faith on the unyielding slopes of Perry County. And it was right that Catholic opulence find a home on the Barrens, where it might stand out the stronger for its surroundings.

No place is this opulence more striking than in the seminary's museums. Near the church is a Visitors' Center and Gift Shop where you may arrange tours. In the adjacent sacristy are ecclesiastical vestments, including that of a Daughter of Charity, which resembles the "Flying Nun" costume. In the seminary's largest building you will see the Countess Estelle Doheny Museum, named for a wealthy Californian whose benefactions earned her a papal title. A rococo hall contains a multitude of fine old porcelains vying with a plethora of paperweights and a bounty of fine books.

The visitor of less exuberant tastes may hope for more congenial exhibits in the second museum, dedicated to the Vincentians' Chinese missions. But the displays here —

ivory figurines, Chinese dolls, wedding headdresses, lots of jade — make the countess' assemblage seem almost Spartan. Even the frou-frou is interesting, however, partly because it is not what you would expect from these heroic missionaries. There are also more traditional displays, like Bishop Rosati's miter and a bell with a royal fleur-de-lis, perhaps a gift of Louis XVIII.

The Rare Book Room, in its way as lavish as the rest, with leaves from the Gutenberg Bible, illuminated medieval manuscripts, and a holograph letter of St. Vincent de Paul, completes the guided visit.

A walk around the grounds is also rewarding. Behind the church is an 1848 red brick building with gallery porches in the back, still occupied by the Vincentians. The adjacent twentieth-century beige brick structures house classrooms no longer in use. The elaborately sheltered cabin southwest of the beige buildings — last of this tour's protected log structures — was built in 1818 for Father Rosati as a sacristy. Notice the simple wooden cross above the entrance; the Barrens' settlers used similar ones over their doors as signs of their Catholicism. A walkway leads south from the cabin to a grotto constructed in the quarry from which the church's stone was taken.

To return to St. Louis, turn right on Missouri 51, which intersects with I-55 a short distance south. Take I-55 north home.

For information call:
Bollinger State Historic Site Mill 1-243-4591
Old McKendree Chapel 1-243-2774
St. Louis Iron Mountain and Southern steam engine 1-243-1688
St. Mary's Seminary 1-547-5761
Trail of Tears State Park 1-334-1711
1845 Trinity Lutheran Church 1-824-5287

Kimmswick

Begins at Interstate 255 and Telegraph Road

Historically America has been too rich to worry about saving, too busy with inventing the new to worry about keeping the old. Just as forests and Indians had to be cleared out for agriculture, so the past and its artifacts have had to make way for the present's aims and profits. Progress meant slash and burn.

But people have come to see that gutted downtowns and tract-house suburbs provide no sense of identity; only an awareness of our roots can do that. Hence the movement for historical preservation.

Good preservation is not simply embalming. Mummification of "historic" villages, for instance, says both too much and too little about history. More interesting are the lively ways the past percolates into the present in Jefferson and Washington counties.

Go south on Telegraph 4.4 miles to Becker where you turn left for Bee Tree Park, marked by a brown sign. After 1.5 miles veer left onto Finestown Road.

Did Bee Tree Park get its name after one of the trees so important to pioneers? That may be the case, but in fact the park is doubly dedicated to the river. Firstly it has superb Mississippi views from the Chubb Overlook. Secondly it has the Golden Eagle Riverboat Museum. That's in the handsome stone house, built in 1929 for Southwestern Bell president Eugene Nims and his wife, the beautiful Franco-Indian Lotawana Flateau.

The museum is an outgrowth of the Golden Eagle Club, founded by three women in 1942 to keep alive the joys of steamboat travel. The Golden Eagle was the last such boat to offer overnight travel out of St. Louis. One of those women, Mrs. Wilbur M. Finger, was on the Eagle when it made what turned out to be its final voyage in 1947; it ran aground near Grand Tower and could not be salvaged.

The museum contains many steamboat models, as well as such memorabilia as anchors, a nine-foot pilot wheel, and an engine room "telegraph" whereby the captain communicated with the engineer. House tours are available for a small fee, and group visits to the museum may be arranged.

Go back to Becker and turn left, south. After a sharp curve Becker ends at Fine Road. Here turn right (north) which after less than a mile brings you back to Telegraph, where you will turn left, south. Cross the Meramec into Jefferson County. Near here in the 1770s, at the mouth of the Meramec, was the first "American" settlement in Missouri — established by Pennsylvania Germans.

Telegraph runs into U.S. 61-67 where you turn left for Imperial. Once in Imperial turn right on Main, cross over Interstate 55, turn right on West Outer Road. Take the second entrance left to the museum of Mastodon State Park.

Mastodons, along with giant ground sloths and long-nosed peccaries, share something of the glamour of the far earlier dinosaur family. As every parent knows, extinct species exert an irresistible fascination over youngsters.

Yet these mastodons have allure for adults too. One theory is that the elephantine beasts were attracted here by mineral springs. But the springs had created a quagmire the mastodons found it hard to get out of; at six or eight tons they were not nimble. Toward the end of the last ice age, about ten thousand years ago, they shared the neighborhood with paleo-Indians known as the Clovis people. The meaty mastodons were an easy target for Clovis hunters.

In fact the archaeological importance of the site rests on the discovery in 1980 of a flint spear head in direct contact with the mastodon bones, offering proof for the first time that man in fact coexisted with mastodons, and perhaps contributed to their extinction.

The discovery would not have been made had real estate developers had their way. What is now the 425-acre state park was about to be sold by the Missouri Highway Department. But four women wanted to conserve the site for future generations. One of them, Dorothy Heinze, explained, "We decided it was a women's world and we were going to prove it." They did. In thirteen months they had raised the purchase price of $568,000, enabling the state to create the park — which has proven enormously popular — and scientists to pursue their research.

The museum's chief exhibit is intended to give the visitor an idea of what it felt like to be near a mastodon. The not yet completed diorama will have a sure scientific basis. The first to exploit the Kimmswick Bone Beds, as the archaeological site here is called, was Albert Koch, who built the bones he found into a huge skeleton he dubbed the Missouri Leviathan. He showed this new type of animal in his museum in St. Louis, then took it on the road in Europe, finally selling it to the British Museum. They reconstructed it into the less fantastic but ever impressive mastodon which still stands in London.

The museum also offers a short slide show. There are a couple of trails in the park, including an easy one from the picnic grounds by a stream watercress-laden in all seasons because it flows from a spring of constant temperature. The bone beds themselves are usually covered over. It is worth negotiating the many steps leading to them only when digging is going on.

Backtrack to Main in Imperial where, at the intersection with U.S. 61 stands a store advertising "Meats Groceries

Pizza Movies Package Liquor Deli Notary Public till after midnite" — a true general store.

Continue straight toward Kimmswick, which means left at the intersection with K, here unmarked.

Like the Golden Eagle Club and Mastodon State Park, tiny Kimmswick owes much to women, in this case one woman in particular, Mrs. Lucianna Gladney Ross. Distressed at the decay and destruction of the village she had known from girlhood, she decided to buy what she could and restore it. Interesting log buildings were brought in from around the region to fill empty spaces. The result is a popular tourist destination, with the quaint shops filled with potpourri and dried flower arrangements that seem the inevitable offspring of the marriage of history and tourism. Two restaurants complete the picture, the Blue Owl, with lovingly prepared desserts, and the Old House, handsomely housed in a transplanted revolutionary-era structure.

Go out of Kimmswick on K to U.S. 61; turn left, and go south for a mile and a half to M. Right on M toward Antonia and Otto through a relatively unspoiled valley with a number of picturesque old farmsteads. Go left (south) on Missouri 21. After 5.9 miles you will see a brown sign for the Sandy Creek Covered Bridge State Historic Site. That means turning left a hundred yards or so after the sign onto Glade Chapel Road, then right at the T in the valley. One of four covered bridges remaining in Missouri, Sandy Creek was one of six that originally stood on the road between Hillsboro and St. Louis. The principal purpose of the covering was to reduce weather damage to the main structure, but such bridges were also reassuring to crossing animals and useful as emergency shelter.

Backtrack to Missouri 21 where you will continue south to Hillsboro, Jefferson County's seat. Turn left at Second Street's stoplight, then right on Hickory, which becomes

Victoria Road at the cemetery. After nearly two and a half miles, just beyond a grouping of houses on the left, lies Victoria Glades Natural Area, managed jointly by the Nature Conservancy and the Missouri Department of Conservation. You may enter only on foot, but be careful. Tarantulas and scorpions, rare this far from the southwest, make their home in these desert-like limestone glades.

Continue on Victoria Road two more miles to Victoria, which has the air of a burg waiting for a train that doesn't stop here any more. The attractive green and white converted depot still stands. Before its railroad days the place achieved a certain notoriety thanks to Prudence Bevis, wife of an early settler and a practitioner of black magic. "Queen Bevers, the Witch" is reported to have turned one of her neighbors into a horse and then to have ridden him to a ball. Twenty-eight years of successful witchery were ended when Henry J. Jones shot an image of Mrs. Bevis with a gun she'd cursed. She subsequently suffered from a sore leg, which earned Jones a magical reputation of his own: ". . . he soon enjoyed a good business counteracting Queen Bever's black magic."[1]

Turn right after the depot on P which takes you south to Missouri 110. Turn right and, after a short distance, left on E, De Soto's Main Street.

Trains do stop in De Soto, where the De Soto car shops look after Union Pacific's cars, as historically they did for Missouri Pacific's. But the town's a tired place, and many of the old buildings that once ennobled its relations with the yards have been torn down. Now De Soto simply stares at the tracks dumbly, not notably heartened that it was the population center of the USA through the 1980s. But along Main Street you see leftward, across the tracks, the Arlington Hotel, and on the right, the Melba, an old cinema, its upper facade of Art Deco tile intact.

Toward the end of Main Street, turn right on Miller.

After the Episcopal Church at Second and the 1885 St. Rose of Lima on Third, Miller becomes N. Follow N's zigzags to Missouri 21 and turn left.

About eight miles south is Washington State Park. Turn right on Missouri 104 into the park's cedar and limestone landscape. Stop for maps and information at the small stone interpretive center, built in the 1930s by an all black CCC unit, as were the other solid stone and timber structures here.

This 1,415-acre park is bordered on the north by the Big River, whose bluffs offer dramatic views. Its most specific attraction is the collection of petroglyphs, shallow symbolic designs Indians carved into the limestone of the glades. The carvings — traces of a truly lost world — are not easy to make out; the clearest ones lie at the end of a walk under a shelter near Missouri 21. Their numbers and the insistent quality inherent in rock carvings hint at a mysterious importance. The Middle Mississippian Indians who made these lightning-throwing thunderbirds and fertility symbols were related to the Cahokia mound builders.

The park is also home to the Missouri Boomer, or collared lizard. This rare glade lover runs upright on his hind legs when agitated. Several splendid trails, swimming and canoeing opportunities, a restaurant and cabins, make this a very complete park.

Exit the park the same way you came in and turn right on Missouri 21. Just over a half mile south is CC. Turn left here for the Old Mines Historical Society.

The world of Washington State Park's petroglyph makers is probably as lost to us as the world of the mastodons and long-nosed peccaries, but at its borders another remote world, that of eighteenth-century France, lives on.

Missouri owes much to Louis XIV. The Sun King's

exhaustion of France's coffers in pursuit of grandeur propelled a frantic search for new resources in the reign of his successor, Louis XV, under whose rule this area was first developed. Word from the Indians that this section of the Mississippi Valley contained mineral wealth, and maps depicting what is now Missouri as practically cheek by jowl with silver-rich Mexico, convinced adventurers and financiers and statesmen that under the reddish soil before you lay the solution to France's debt.

Silver was what they hoped for, but lead is what they got. Lead has plenty of uses, but that of replenishing the French purse was not among them.

Frenchmen and French-Canadians came here all the same. With their picks and shovels and little else, these men might seem even further from the court of Louis XV than lead is from silver. But despite all that separated them, they did share a culture. Astonishingly, something of that culture has survived.

Survival against the odds is always heartening, perhaps because we half-consciously sense that if they could do it, so can we. Survival of Old France in a supposedly homogenized society like ours is especially a cause for glee.

One account of the twentieth-century Creole tells how he works a little in his garden plot, and a little more on his diggings, the shallow pits whose ore offered a meager subsistence. "Often the miner gathers enough ore during the first half of the week to permit him to hunt or fish or doze upon his *galerie* until the following Monday."[2]

That description was written in the 1930s; this kind of hand mining ceased in the 1980s. But hereabouts people still take their ancient sporting pastimes, as well as their good food, good music, and good dancing, very seriously — just as the court at Versailles did. A local saying has it that all you need for a party here is a shade tree, two Frenchmen, and a jug of wine.

That people should be attached to this world is not surprising. Modern Creoles may not have a great deal of money; jobs are scarce. But they have accomplished something. "Their success is largely the retention of their culture," scholar Ray Brassieur puts it. "They are rich in that."[3] Even though Missouri French is now the first language of only a couple dozen older people, interest in the French heritage and attachment to home and family are still strong.

Such tenacity has side effects. At times French Missourians appear reluctant to assume bigger work responsibilities — perhaps because to do so might take them away from their Gallic hearths. Unwillingness to move may also be related to the surrounding culture's past intolerance. Missouri observer Henry Schoolcraft in 1819 wrote of this area that "The French constitute a considerable portion of the whole population, and it is but repeating a commonplace to say, that in morality and intelligence they are inferior to the American population."[4] American scorn for the foreign meant that children were forbidden to speak French in public school.

Fortunately creole culture continues to have solid points of reference. The very active Old Mines Historical Society keeps its archives and some of its memorabilia in the small wood structure here in the hamlet of Fertile. Also on the grounds on CC, just off Missouri 21, are an old white schoolhouse, an interesting log cabin, and mining and agricultural tools.

Just beyond on CC stands the 1876 brick home of the Rural Parish Workers, dedicated Catholic laywomen who came here in the late 1940s. Their apostolate includes preservation of local creole culture; it is one aspect of their effort "to restore all things in Christ." The group, whose services to their community are innumerable and much appreciated, has energetically supported the

Historical Society since its 1977 beginnings.

Return to Missouri 21 and go left, south. About two miles from CC — or exactly one mile from the southern entrance to Washington State Park — is a gravel road. Turn right on it and right again at the first opportunity. At the dead end of this short spur is Cannon Mines Creek. "No country can be more plentifully watered, possessing in great abundance the most delightful fountains and rivulets," Schoolcraft reminds us.[5]

Just to the right stands the high stone chimney of Murphy's Furnace. Of almost Roman monumentality, it dates from the first decade of the nineteenth century. The non-French name is significant; technological advances in mining processes were linked to English-speaking newcomers here. Schoolcraft remarked that "The Creoles never smelted any other way than by throwing the lead on log heaps."[6] Look through its arched opening. Another stone chimney sits nearer the highway.

Return to Missouri 21 and turn right, continuing south into Old Mines, a community described as "accumulated rather than founded."[7] Nancy's Restaurant, on the left beyond the junction of Missouri 21 and Missouri 47, though it may not look like much — nothing does in Old Mines — should be noted for its live music on weekends.

About five miles south of the meeting of Missouri 21 and 47, the focus of Old Mines appears on the right: the Church of St. Joachim, built in 1828 with additions after the middle of the century. Inside is a copper bucket, the baptismal font of earlier days. Note the iron crosses in the cemetery to the south, as well as the graves of Monsieur and Madame LaMarque (a Bolduc from Ste Genevieve), benefactors of St. Joachim. The white structure with its gallery porch facing Missouri 21 is their 1810 house. The clapboards cover vertical log construction, a method used in Old Mines into the twentieth century.

Also visible from the church are a group of log cabins belonging to another Old Mines cultural institution, La Brigade à Renault, named for the man who first directed mining operations for Louis XV in this area. La Brigade's most spectacular interest lies in recreating pre-1840 black powder shoots with campsites and costumes as historically accurate as the explosives. They also sponsor the *Fête l'Automne* every October.

Backtrack north on Missouri 21 to Missouri 47 and turn left. Approximately eight miles west, turn left on A. Just opposite the turn a wooden sign calls Richwoods a 1770s French village. The ore of this area may in fact have been exploited by miners from Old Mines at that date, but the village itself was not founded until the 1830s. Nonetheless more than any community except Ste Genevieve it has the creole look, evidenced by the haphazard siting of most of the buildings, the numerous gallery porches, and the old log structures.

Note the Methodist mud-stucco church to the left about a half mile down A. Farther on and to the right are two vaguely creole cottages. They're set back beyond the creek which perhaps drew settlers to this site. Behind the Sassy Skillet Cafe, part of Richwoods' downtown, is a log dwelling.

Just out of town is St. Stephen's Church, not beautiful except in its siting, neatness, and windows. Toussaint Charbonneau, husband of Lewis and Clark's Sacajawea, is said to be buried in the old graveyard on a slope to the right of the church.

Backtrack across Missouri 47, where A becomes H. Note how mining has scarred this landscape. After a little over three miles, turn left, north, on WW. At the intersection with Y, turn left through Grubville, whose food co-op attracts ecological utopians.

Ten miles beyond, Missouri 30 appears; turn right.

After thirteen miles, turn left on W toward Eureka. 6.5 miles later, veer left on FF: W continues to the right. FF ends at F. Turn left across La Barque Creek, and, shortly beyond, right at the sign for St. Joseph Hills. Drive less than half a mile to the entrance to the Black Madonna Shrine, on the left.

The scene at the top of the steep driveway is at first uninspiring. But the carport is really a chapel with no less than three reproductions of the Black Madonna of Czestochowa. Behind it is a procession of grottos.

Brother Bronislaus, a Polish Franciscan, built this shrine in his free time. The eccentric fervor which saw him through years of construction produced an architectural fantasy of sandcastle zaniness. Fake-jewel and cafeteria-china mosaics are background to white plaster saints. Urns of cacti and flowers are shaped out of mortar and colored gravel. Porcelain birds collected at church bazaars flock around St. Francis. Everything from kneelers to niches is covered in barite rocks; from a distance it all looks as though it might be made of peanut brittle.

The kind of colorful Catholicism which produced shrines like this has all but disappeared in the United States.

Backtrack on F to FF and then to W. Turn left on W and follow it across the Meramec to Eureka where you pick up Interstate 44 east.

The most truly lost of all these worlds is Times Beach, which appears next to you on I-44, a Meramec River community abandoned in 1983 after its roads were accidentally sprayed with dioxin.

For information call:
Bee Tree Park 889-2454
Golden Eagle Riverboat Museum 846-9073
Mastodon State Park Museum 1-464-2976
Old Mines Historical Society 1-586-5171, ask for Alice Widmer
Washington State Park 1-586-2995

Bonne Terre depot

Begins at exit 180 for Pevely, Interstate 55; turn left (east)
for U.S. 67; turn right (south) on U.S. 67

". . . the lands are reputed to equal in fertility the banks
of the Nile, and the mountains to vie with the wealth of
Peru."[1] This view of the Mississippi valley could not
help but impress the early-eighteenth-century court of
Versailles, deeply in debt from the Sun King's splendid
reign.

Enthusiastic arrangements to exploit the region's mineral riches culminated in the Mississippi Bubble. This
scheme, elaborated by Scottish financier John Law, entailed his company's assumption of the French national
debt, among other things. In exchange the Compagnie
des Indes acquired a near monopoly on France's foreign
trade. Law's success depended on two things: his stock-
holders' patience, and a quick return on his New World
mining investments. The latter, in turn, depended on
striking silver. But the only silver they "found" was in
an initial ore test which appears to have been fudged.
Missouri offered only lead — not a metal designed to
impress French investors. The Bubble burst.

Others who mined Missouri fared better; this tour
takes you into the Old Mineral Belt they developed.
Here, since the eighteenth century, the mining industry
and mining communities have existed in a sometimes
gracious, sometimes brutal symbiosis.

As you head south on U.S. 67, note on the right the
Pevely flea market, situated in a drive-in movie theater.

A bit farther south, also on the right, is the 1863 white stone Landmark Manor.

Soon after a brown sign directs you left on Joachim Street for the Fletcher Dunklin Historic Site. Stay left on Main Street, which runs along the bluffs.

You have entered Herculaneum, founded by Moses Austin in 1808. Apparently the site's sedimentary bluffs reminded Austin of the recently excavated town buried with Pompeii by Vesuvius' 79 A.D. eruption. Like the ancient town, Austin's Herculaneum was to be a port; he needed a shipping point nearer his Potosi mines than Ste Genevieve.

As it turned out, Herculaneum became more than a port. The bluffs were perfect foundations for shot towers. From these structures molten lead was dropped through a copper sieve and let fall between 90 and 140 feet, depending on the size shot desired, into a cistern of water. A rolling barrel then polished the rough droplets smooth. Along with lead and shot, the port shipped lumber, gunpowder, meats, grains, and whiskey.

Stop at the Fletcher Dunklin site; here were the shot towers. To the right, a grand presence between the bluffs and the river, is the Doe Run lead smelting plant. Proceed toward it down Main, then turn right on Station, which becomes Brown as it curves right. Turn left at the second stop sign. Joachim leads back to U.S. 67.

Go left (south) on U.S. 67 about a hundred yards. Turn left on Riverview at the sign for the Ursuline Convent — we're not going there but it is near the road we follow south. Turn right on Mississippi Avenue. At the T intersection, turn left on Crystal Heights, which winds into Crystal City.

Here successive shorelines of primeval seas reworked quartz crystals into an ever finer white sand, ideal for glass manufacturing. A Detroit glassmaker began production in 1872 — and called this spot New Detroit.

The transformation of sand to glass impressed Walt Whitman during a visit in 1879: "a wonderful process, a real poem . . . all glowing, a newer vaster study for the Colorists, indescribable, a pale red-tinged yellow, of tarry consistence all lambent . . . sometimes sun striking it from above with effect that would have filled Michel Angelo with rapture."[2]

New Detroit became Crystal City when Pittsburgh Plate Glass purchased the sand deposits in the 1890s and built a company town.

Turn left on Mississippi opposite the brick high school and left again opposite the elementary school. Crystal City's orderliness, the brick streets, the overarching trees, the pretty stone church tucked into a park, all manifest the company's paternalistic desire to structure employee life. The effort extended to morality: Crystal City was not only a company town, it was a dry company town. Turn right on Bailey just after Grace Presbyterian Church.

Bailey leads toward Festus, just across the tracks. This town, which we do not visit, was the result of weary workers' desire to have a good time. That meant escape from the orderly procession between factory and family. Festus, originally called Tanglefoot, was wet from the beginning. Even now its Main Street, visible from the intersection of Bailey and U.S. 67 (Truman Boulevard), has a kind of honky-tonk vitality.

West of Festus is mined the sand that Pittsburgh Plate Glass uses to manufacture eighty million square feet of glass a year at its Crystal City plant.

Go south on U.S. 67 toward Bonne Terre. On the left, after about twenty miles, is St. Francois State Park. Note the signs along the highway beyond — Mineral Area Kitchens, Mineral Area College, Mineral Area Realty and Lead Belt Pentecostal Church. The region is sure of its identity.

Exit right onto Missouri 47. After you enter Bonne Terre, go to the top of a slight rise. Turn left, opposite Monterey Mushrooms, on Summit Street. This takes you through an area formerly known as Hunky Hill, now just the Hill. Early-twentieth-century Slovak and Hungarian immigrants lived here in company houses, each with its own cow barn. Workers bought these $750 homes with payments of $2 a week.

Locals felt threatened by the inhabitants of Hunky Hill; they accused the company of replacing Americans with foreign labor at lower wages. The tension came to a head on July 13, 1917. After a burst of violence in which several immigrants were pushed from second story windows, American miners herded their foreign colleagues to the company cashier for a check, then to the bank for cash and finally to the train station.

The Americans softened at the depot. Long time foreign residents of Bonne Terre were allowed to stay. Women and children could remain in their homes until their menfolk found work elsewhere. The rioters even passed the hat to collect train fare for one large family.

But industrial relations here were mostly peaceful. St. Joseph Minerals, who laid out Bonne Terre in 1880 and whose headquarters were here until 1962, had an especially fine reputation with its employees. As one man put it, "Once you got a job at St. Joe's you had a job for life unless you screwed up something good." Fruitful relations went beyond the workplace. Bonne Terre was a complete company town: St. Joe provided stores, houses, a library, a hospital and a water system.

The care that went into town planning is still evident. After St. Joe's departure pessimists expected Bonne Terre to disappear. But there was too much life for the town simply to wither. Some people left, but those who remain are committed to the place; they have undertaken a campaign to have the city listed on the National Register of Historic Places.

At Summit and Oak follow the signs left for Mansion Hill Country Inn and Restaurant, originally built as an executive residence. Note the chat piles in the distance both north and south as well as the donkeys and peacocks in the yard.

Exit and stay left on Oak. On the left is the luxurious stone and frame house of the General Manager of the operations here. Both these homes for high-ups are on hills.

Before Oak crosses the railroad tracks, note William's Crusher, one of the industries occupying St. Joe Lead Company's old sheds, which extend almost to Missouri 47.

Across the tracks is the spiffily restored 1909 Bonne Terre Depot. The turret served as the roundhouse. The depot had two waiting rooms: one for executives and their wives, the other for laborers.

Veer right across from the depot on Allen, which takes you to the town square. The English-style brick and stone building is the old St. Joe headquarters. Next door, appropriately enough, was the town's first bank. The stone building now houses an insurance agency. The blue and white building across the square was called the Club House. Single managers and engineers lived here with a cook and caretaker. It is now a bed and breakfast inn. To its left is the white house of the St. Joe treasurer.

Continue to Main Street Northeast and turn left. At the stop sign look right for the Lamplighter Inn, where good food is served except on Sundays and Mondays, when it is closed.

Cross the intersection for Main Street Northwest. There is a turn-of-the-century stone library on the corner. It came by its monumental air honestly: it originally was a monument — to one J. Wyman Jones, an early St. Joe Lead Company official.

Behind the library you glimpse a Tudor-style building, according to townspeople an enlarged version of Shakespeare's house. The St. Joe executive who planned this brick and stucco assemblage as a company store was warned that miners wouldn't shop in so fancy a place. He built it anyway; the miners wouldn't shop there. It is now City Hall.

Next door to the library is the Shepard House, the first frame building in Bonne Terre. Here lived Charles Bunyan Parsons, a Michigan dentist who revolutionized Missouri mining with his 1869 introduction of the diamond drill. The new drill increased the company's production drastically; by 1900 St. Joe's was the largest lead company in southeastern Missouri.

Continue down Main. These big frame houses were financed by St. Joe for its married executives. Note tiny stone St. Peter's Church.

Make a sharp right onto Division and right again on School Street East; this is downtown. Follow the arrow for Missouri 47. Turn right into the Bonne Terre Mine.

You may visit the world's largest man-made cavern. The underground space itself is more impressive than some of its alleged attractions. The underground flower garden, for instance, consists of a few houseplants under a grow light.

The strongest draw is something you would never expect in a town called Good Earth: scuba diving. When mining operations ceased, so did the pumps. A million gallons filled the abyss — creating a new resource for the town.

You might think this has little to do with mining. Publicists assure us that history is what the dives are all about. Divers in fact can see a foreman's shack under eighty feet of water, loaded ore cars on the mines' railroad tracks, rock drills, ladders, and soggy newspapers.

The mine entrance is surrounded by western-style storefronts denominated museum, cafe, company store, barber shop and post office. The last two have period interiors. In the parking lot are a few pieces of mining equipment painted Pepto-Bismol colors.

Go right at the mine exit, and right again at the stop sign on Allen Street South. Just behind the tall beige frame building (the original Masonic Lodge) is an interesting white structure built as a library. The library became a pool house when St. Joe constructed a swimming pool where the parking lot now is. The townspeople still call the building the natatorium. The pool was emptied and refilled once a week with pumpings from the mine. It was scrapped when health authorities insisted on a filtering system.

Note the tiny depot-like building across Allen from the Masonic lodge.

Turn right onto Main St. Northeast. Cross the intersection and veer left onto Church Street, named for the First Congregational Church on your left, a reduced scale model of an English church. Bonne Terre's builders clearly thought British styles the most appropriate for public buildings. Church Street has more executive housing.

At the intersection of Church, Shepherd and Lake, curve left with Lake Street. You'll immediately pass the company-built yellow brick hospital.

Follow Lake out of town. You will pass two cruel-looking industrial facilities on the left. Go right on business 67, which twists through Desloge and Flat River. Beyond the latter's downtown, just after the top of a rise, is Federal Mill Road. Turn right for the Missouri Mines State Historic Site. (Directions will change with the planned extension of Missouri 32; after construction ends, the museum entrance will be at Missouri 32 and Chestnut.) East of the site once stood the world's largest chat pile.

The site itself was Federal Lead Company's Mill No. 3, a powerful presence on its wind-swept height. Built in 1906 as an ore concentrating plant, it was purchased by St. Joseph's in 1923. Ore taken from the nearly one thousand miles of undergound passages in this area was hoisted to the surface via an impressive headframe through a shaft excavated from the bottom up. Mining activity here — and in the Old Lead Belt in general — stopped in 1972 when St. Joe moved to Viburnum and the New Lead Belt.

In 1976 the company transferred more than 8,500 acres to the state, which became St. Joe State Park. In 1980 twenty-five acres were separated as the Missouri Mines State Historic Site. Opened officially in May 1988, the site is still being developed. Mineral exhibits, including one of fluorescent minerals, mining equipment, and a dated but ecologically revealing St. Joe promotional film will be joined soon by a gallery devoted to the history of Missouri mining. There is an attractive gift shop.

Backtrack north on business 67 to Missouri 8, which you follow west to Potosi.

The Indians mined here for flints, clay, and iron oxide used in war paint. The French, in response to Law's grand vision, began their digging around 1720. They were not much more systematic than the Indians, who sometimes harassed them. But director of the mines Philippe Renault did show how productive the area could be. At their peak, Renault's operations are reported to have smelted 1,500 pounds of lead a day.

That figure notwithstanding, French mining methods failed to take full advantage of the area's mineral resources. As Schoolcraft, commenting on creole mining years later, put it, "In general there is a greater disposition to trust to luck and chance, and stumble upon ore, than by attending to mineral character, to be sure of success."[3]

Potosi was the product of just such stumbling. A former employee of Renault, François Azau, whose creole nickname was le Breton, discovered a surface deposit of lead while bear hunting in 1774. It turned out to be the richest site around. The village established here in the early 1790s, called Mine à Breton, became the first European settlement located any distance west of the Mississippi.

Mine à Breton's casual French mining mode was soon transformed. In 1796, a Connecticut Yankee with long experience in the lead business crossed the Mississippi to get a land grant in the lead belt. Moses Austin shrewdly judged St. Louis' Spanish officials. "I have it from his own lips," Schoolcraft reports, "that . . . he thought it necessary to enter the town with as large a retinue, and as much parade as possible. He led the way himself, on the best horse he could muster, clothed in a long blue mantle, lined with scarlet and embroidered with lace, and rode through the principal street, where the Governor resided, followed by his servants, guides, and others . . . . The favourable impression created by this *entrée* . . . led on to his ultimate success."[4] Austin got a square league of ground around what, in 1814, became Potosi.

Austin's shrewdness extended beyond real estate into modernizing the lead industry. He sank the first mine shaft — the French dug only shallow pits. He set up the first reverberatory furnace; he founded Herculaneum. But the post-Napoleonic depression of the 1810s put an end to his numerous successes. The Bank of St. Louis went broke, and that in turn bankrupted Austin.

This misfortune spurred him to new enterprise. Texas' Spanish governor granted him the right to settle with three hundred American families there. But Austin died before he could carry out the venture. His son

Stephen, the Father of Texas, was to do it for him.

Nineteenth-century Potosi was home to another distinguished family. The Desloges, St. Joseph Lead Company owners and great benefactors of this area of Missouri, arrived in 1823.

Other mining fortunes were made here more recently when Potosi became the world's barite capital. Barite, also called tiff, is found with lead; it is used in oil drilling and as a paint stabilizer.

Missouri 8 crosses Missouri 21 at Potosi's edge. Continue west for M Street where you turn right. Turn left a block later on Breton. At Mine Street note the 1908 stone church, designed by the dean of American black architects, John Anderson Lankfor, whose parents were slaves in Potosi. Catercorner stands an elaborate brown and beige Victorian house, now property of the Mine à Breton Historical Society. This structure's fine porch is the first of Potosi's notable verandas. Continue on Breton past the white 1848 Temperance and Opera House, now a Masonic Lodge, to the 1832 red brick Presbyterian Church, oldest standing Presbyterian church west of the Mississippi, home of the Historical Society. Behind and to the right of the church is Moses Austin's grave — a whitewashed adobe-esque affair illuminated by an ever-burning gas lamp. Texans sent an undertaker to crack open the tomb and bring Austin to Texas in 1938. After the man was discovered, Texas' Secretary of State delivered Potosi a formal apology from the Governor.

Beyond the church turn right on Mineral, and right again on Market. Note the one of a kind porch at Market and Mine. Turn right at Missouri Street. On the left is the attractive 1859 St. James Church; its more recent interior is graced by octagonal oak columns, an oak ceiling, and bright stained glass windows.

Cross Missouri 8, heading down the narrow continuation of Missouri Street. Just before the creek is what remains of Moses Austin's 1798 Durham Hall, "the cradle of Texas," which was destroyed in an 1871 fire. Cross the creek — here was the original Mine à Breton settlement. Turn right on Jefferson, which runs near pleasant Breton Creek.

Turn left on Missouri 8, then quickly right onto Missouri 185. After the plaster cows which appear to your right, you're in beautiful countryside interrupted only by an abandoned plant ten miles out of Potosi. Ten miles farther look left for a very active plant in the distance. Turn left two and a half miles beyond on EE for the Pea Ridge Iron Ore Company.

Mining produces towns like Bonne Terre and Potosi; its wealth helps protect forests like the one you have just driven through. But there is a cost. As you approach the facility you see vast dead gray stretches. Here Pea Ridge spreads its tailings — what's left after the refining process.

Return to Missouri 185. Turn left (west) for Sullivan where you can pick up Interstate 44 east for St. Louis.

For information call:
Bonne Terre Mine 1-358-2148
Missouri Mines State Historic Site 1-431-6226
St. Joe State Park 1-431-1069

Elephant Rock State Park

Take Interstate 55 south, then U.S. 67 south to begin at
Missouri 72

Minerals have dictated much of the history of the area
southwest of St. Louis. In some instances, like the portion
of St. Joe State Park set aside as a sort of Bonneville Flats
for recreational vehicles, their presence has meant a landscape scarred beyond redemption. But elsewhere, even
in places as exploited as the lead belt, the region's beauty
has survived man's tampering. Some of the loveliest
scenery in the state lies near mines and quarries.

At about sixty miles south of Interstate 270, U.S. 67
passes near Farmington, the seat of St. Francois County.
If you're a nineteenth-century architecture buff, you
may want to detour here. The little city has a series of
well-landscaped, well-maintained Victorian houses at
nos. 314, 324, 502, 503, 513, 604 and 628 West Columbia.
Exit U.S. 67 on W east, which is Columbia, and follow it
to the courthouse which you will loop around, backtracking then to U.S. 67.

Continue sixteen and a half miles south on U.S. 67 to
Missouri 72, which you take west toward Arcadia. Missouri 72 rolls through scenery that a romantic landscape
painter might have composed. Eight miles west of U.S. 67
is the entrance to the Millstream Gardens State Forest
where the St. Francis River passes through a rocky formation known as a shut-in. Spring water levels make
the stream perfect for whitewater boating; races have
been held every spring for twenty-two years.

Once in the park, follow the arrow for river access. When the road forks, take the left branch for Tiemann Shut-Ins; you pass a crumbling log cabin. It's a pleasant quarter mile stroll from the new picnic shelter by a pretzeled evergreen and over the Deer Run covered bridge to the shut-ins. Spring wildflowers are spectacular here.

After seventeen miles Missouri 72 intersects with Missouri 21, which you will take north, passing by Ironton for now. Turning right a short distance beyond Ironton at V, you come to a hexagonal earthen redoubt. This is Fort Davidson, built in the shadow of Pilot Knob in 1863.

Missouri suffered more from the Civil War than any other state, except perhaps Virginia and Tennessee. This was partly because of Missourians' high rate of participation; 60 percent of eligible males took up arms, a figure unequalled by any other state. What perhaps motivated them, even as it intensified Missouri's suffering, was the fissure in the state's sympathies. The government in Jefferson City in fact opted for the Confederacy, and only the vigor of unionists, especially of the many new German Missourians, kept the state from joining the south.

It is hard to imagine Pilot Knob's peaceful and even idyllic landscape as a setting for bloodshed, but one of the war's fiercest confrontations took place here.

The Battle of Pilot Knob might not have happened. True, the iron deposits here, the railway, and the fort's proximity to St. Louis gave Pilot Knob a certain importance. But by 1864 the war's real action was elsewhere; this was the year of Sherman's march through Georgia to the sea.

Precisely that ferocious southeastern action moved Kirby Smith, the Confederacy's Trans-Mississippi commanding general, to look for a pretext *not* to send troops there. Smith wanted to save his infantry — for defense of his own area. As a cover for this selfishness he sent Jefferson Davis word that he was planning a major western campaign.

The hastily organized "campaign" had as its final goal poorly-garrisoned St. Louis. Leading the Confederacy's twelve thousand troops was Sterling Price, a former governor of Missouri.

His men were underequipped; one writer called the best of them "gallant ragamuffins." But they outnumbered the federal troops more than ten to one. Union district commander Thomas Ewing had orders to fall back on St. Louis if rebel numbers at Pilot Knob were overwhelming. But Ewing and his officers decided that they could hold the fort.

Their hope was soon tested; Price's troops managed fairly quickly to push back the northerners. But as the battle began in earnest the afternoon of September 27, 1864, the advantages of Fort Davidson's position on the plain became clear. As the solid walls of Southern footsoldiers advanced within range, federal rifles mowed them down like "wheat straw before a scythe."[1]

Despite enormous losses, the Rebels kept coming; Union defenders had to abandon the rifle pits for the fort. Now the Confederate brigades stormed forward, soon filling the dry moats.

Here the worst took place; Union gunners lobbed grenades onto the massed soldiers. As a captain from Iowa described it, "Men were blown above the parapet and fell back dead; the ditches were cleared as if by magic. It struck terror to the enemy's lines, and they fell back in disorder . . . "[2]

Within twenty minutes dead and wounded men covered the five hundred yards before the fort. The Confederacy lost 1,200 men here, the Union 200 — a carnage making Pilot Knob one of the bloodiest battles of

America's bloodiest war.

As night settled on the Arcadia Valley, Ewing realized he had a problem. However damaged Price had been, by the next morning the Confederates would have artillery in place on Shephard Mountain. How could they hold out against bombardment from above? Ewing decided to attempt an escape. He mustered his weary men in the moat on the dark side of the fort. Muffling the artillery wheels with canvas, they slipped silently northward, making it safely through the Confederates' loose lines.

A rear guard, before quitting the fort, then lit a fuse. It led to the well-stocked powder magazine. ". . . suddenly the heavens were lighted up by a grand column of fire ascending hundreds of feet . . . making the whole region reverberate with the sound as though a mighty thunderbolt had riven Pilot's Knob," wrote Missouri soldier Thomas Fletcher.[3]

The Confederates thought the blast was an accident. The next morning Price was enraged to find Fort Davidson empty, a smoking pit where the magazine had been. The fort, the town, the mines, and the railroad were now all his. But just as Ewing had kept ammunition out of Rebel hands, so had he sent all locomotives and rolling stock to safety. This, with the delay the battle entailed, meant Union reinforcements had time to reach St. Louis. Price's troops had been decimated; a Confederate St. Louis was now out of the question.

The tired army turned northwest toward Jefferson City, where they were no more effective than they had been at Pilot Knob. Less than a month later, near Kansas City, they met their final defeat in the Battle of Westport.

Pilot Knob's crown is scarred from mining. Now the last pieces of equipment are being removed. In the 1840s people were convinced that this and neighboring Iron Mountain were made of solid ore, and could supply the world with iron for a century. In 1843 a plank road to Ste Genevieve was built so that the metal might be shipped more efficiently.

The Iron Mountain Railroad to St. Louis replaced this route in the late 1850s and encouraged development of the valley's towns. Ease of transportation to the city and the intact beauty of much of the valley attracted builders of summer homes to the area.

Take Missouri 21 south less than a mile. A small white sign for Ironton's Business District directs you left onto Main Street. Take the second right, Polk Street, and then turn left on Shepherd. Here are some pleasant stone (the spongy-looking stone is barite) and frame bungalows, mixed with a few nineteenth-century homes.

At Reynolds and Shepherd, glance at the unusually crafted Ironton Assembly of God. Across Reynolds sits an 1886 steamboat Gothic wonder, topped by an elaborate widow's walk.

Turn left on Reynolds and continue two blocks to Knob Street to see the 1870 St. Paul's Episcopal Church, a winning Victorian Gothic wood structure, with a splashy roof and wooden pinnacles. The interior of this thoroughly fine structure is warm but dignified. Note the decorative roof supports, the hand-painted window high on the entrance wall, and the stenciling — garden flowers and farm crops — of the other windows.

A left on Knob Street takes you past St. Paul's frame parsonage with its diagonal porch, also on the left. After an eccentric brick structure turn left on Madison. Go left down Main two blocks to the 1858 Iron County courthouse, used as hospital and barracks during the conflict. Its east and south facades are pock-marked from Confederate firing. Note the Turkish crescent moon and star motif of the turn-of-the-century gazebo.

Across Wayne Street from the courthouse is the

Ironton County Historical Museum which has, among other memorabilia, the tatters of a Confederate flag from the Battle of Pilot Knob.

A right on Russell (M) will take you by the brick sheriff's house, on the square, and its adjoining limestone block jail, both built in 1866. Follow Russell, with its substantial homes, keeping right at the fork for no. 711, Chanticleer Ceramics.

Dr. T.R. Goulding built this cheerfully eclectic house in 1872 as both home and office. The neighboring stone building, which you glimpse to the left of the driveway, was his hospital. The civic-minded Gould purchased the white statues here for the courthouse grounds, but they were deemed too revealing for public consumption.

Back at the fork, look right across the field for the double porches of the 1873 brick home nestled in a grove of trees.

Backtrack to Main Street where a right takes you into adjacent Arcadia. Continue two miles or so to East Maple Street and turn left, then right into the gate of the red brick Ursuline Academy. Preceded here by a Southern Methodist boys' school founded in 1849, the same year as Arcadia, the now all but abandoned academy has a nostalgic air befitting its southern background. Follow the drive counterclockwise past the gymnasium, church and main building, then right behind the complex and out again onto Main. Turn right, and backtrack through Arcadia to the stop sign just after Elm. A right here will bring you to Missouri 21, which you take right again, southward, unless you want to eat a bite at Whistle Junction, the former depot.

Outside Arcadia begins the gradual ascent to Taum Sauk Mountain, at 1,722 feet the highest point in Missouri. "Mountain" is no more than a courtesy title for the gentle eminences that make up most of the Ozarks. But the Boston chain in Arkansas and the St. Francois Mountains here do deserve the term. If they lack the obvious superficial visual drama of western mountains, they make up for it with a far longer and more complex history.

What first created the Ozark highland is not known. What is known is that the Ozarks' geological center, the St. Francois Mountains, is distinguished by surface rocks a billion and a half years old. The Rockies date from a mere 250 million years ago.

These rarely found rocks were produced when the earth's internal fires blasted through a still older surface, creating volcanos. But a billion years of erosion flattened what had begun as towering mountains. Then, half a billion years ago, successive inundations — from the Arctic or what is now the Gulf — began covering the area. These seas deposited layers of dolomite, limestone, sandstone and shale over the granite and porphyry extrusions of the first mountains. Uplift and erosion of the whole region alternated with submersion and sedimentation.

Subsequently, in a very few places, the limestone layers eroded away sufficiently to expose the igneous rocks of the original mountain range, rocks that elsewhere constitute the deep geological "basement" of the area. The St. Francois Mountains are one of these places.

If Ozark geological history is complex, so is its social history. Missouri 21 takes you past some stereotypical Ozark homesteads: bare dirt yards, pigs, porches and old cars. An intriguing explanation for this picturesque but often disconcerting lifestyle is that the Ozarks constitute a semi-arrested frontier.

The American frontier, the most important factor in our nineteenth-century social geography, was always moving and therefore always offering Americans a chance for a different life. Nothing about it was permanent, for nothing was to interfere with the possibility of progress.

The Ozarks present the unusual spectacle of a land where, like the frontier, little is permanent, yet not much seems to change. The hills still offer many of the advantages of the frontier. Game is plentiful, civilization's restrictions few. The poor quality of the soil means that real farms are rare; settlers could not put down the deep roots that make for stability. But that's good for hunting — too much cow and plow discourages wildlife.

The population is largely of Scotch-Irish extraction. Even before crossing the Atlantic, many Scotch-Irish lived in an unsettled relation to their environment. In Scotland they fought with Celtic Highlanders and in Ireland with the Irish. Many who emigrated were forest dwellers, poachers, charcoal burners and the like, as Leonard Hall in his beautiful *Stars Upstream* points out. This gave them an advantage on the frontier. "They came naturally by their ability as woodsmen." But it also gave them a "spirit of utter independence," and a "disregard for authority as represented by game laws, grazing regulations, and absentee ownership of timber."[4]

A little over four and a half miles to the south is CC. A right on it leads up to Taum Sauk's peak. Here there is a surprise: no view. But if you climb the fire tower you'll see what the gentle, rolling Ozarks are about — the grace of age.

This mountain and much of what you see are becoming part of a greatly expanded Johnson's Shut-Ins State Park. Taum Sauk's slopes feature a seasonal waterfall, Mina Sauk. Mina, daughter of Taum, was one of those star-crossed Indian lovers so often paired with rude escarpments in American geography.

Backtrack to Missouri 21 and turn right through Royal Gorge. Less than four miles south of CC is AA.

Unspoiled nature is this tour's principal attraction. But you may want to detour on AA to see a mountaintop reservoir built by Union Electric in the early 1960s. Here nature has been made to serve man: the top of Profitt Mountain is now a walled fifty-five acre reservoir. Its unremitting bleakness is not without dramatic effect. When you turn your back to the concrete there are magnificent Ozark views. The site may be visited from March through November; there is a small natural resources museum. From here you may rejoin Missouri 21 via unmarked U — maps are available at the museum — where you turn right toward Lesterville.

If you do not want to take the time to visit the electric plant, follow Missouri 21 south. Just before it curves sharply right, you will see the concrete stacks — one is 610 feet high — of Asarco's 1966 lead smelting plant at Glover. Follow Missouri 21 five and a half miles to Lesterville.

Veer left onto Lesterville's barely paved Main Street, which boasts, on the left, the Double Trouble Waterslide, formerly "800 feet of pure excitement." Main Street is also not too alive. At the cluster of vacant storefronts look left; one block off sits a white frame house with a double gallery porch. After the Baptist Church turn right on Parks and left on Missouri 21. Less than two and a half miles beyond, turn right on N, which passes through the Johnson's Shut-Ins State Park. Go right on MM to the visitors area, from which a quarter mile walk takes you to an overlook.

After thick layers of sedimentary rock were deposited on the Ozarks' hard igneous underpinning, this whole region was uplifted. Ozark streams began a 250-million-year process of slicing through the relatively soft sedimentary covering to the igneous rock underneath. The resistant igneous layer erodes slowly, usually along fracture lines, confining the streams into narrow gorges called shut-ins.

The overlook provides a view of the Pothole Shut-In, so named for the many pools hollowed out by the East Fork of the Black River.

The Pothole Shut-In's intricate network of overflowing pools, narrow spillways, and rounded stepping stones reactivates the childhood fascination for dams and moving water. The temptation to leave the observation deck and step from rock to rock over torrents is almost irresistible. As the signs here suggest, though, you should exercise caution or you'll end up wet — at the very least.

Follow the hiking trail a hundred yards or so beyond the Pothole Shut-In. At the top of the rise you look down into a clear pool of blue green water flanked by a bluff of red granite and porphyry. Seen on bright winter days it is as beautiful as Capri. In fact winter is the best time to see Johnson's Shut-Ins; summer foliage overpowers the reds and pinks of the rocks and the grey-greens of the lichens. In cool afternoon light the views here achieve the delicate surrealism of old hand-tinted postcards.

The park's original 2,000 acres were gathered over seventeen years by Joseph Desloge who made it a gift to Missouri in 1955. The Desloge family, who arrived in Potosi in 1823, became owners of the St. Joseph Lead Company. Nineteen ninety expansion is enlarging the park to over 6,000 acres.

Back on N, turn right through a grassy valley. After thirteen miles, turn left on Missouri 21. A half mile later, veer left onto RA. Elephant Rocks State Park is on the right. An interpretive shelter explains the phenomenon you are about to see — but leave that for last and take the paved trail, organized for blind and seeing visitors. We suggest a clockwise route with an easy rock descent at the end for the appropriately shod. Like the shut-ins, Elephant Rocks is best in winter, when the boulders nestled in the woods look like resting animals and the great pink rocks can be clearly seen.

The path leads gently upward to a steep-walled quarry, its deep waters reflecting a scene of oriental composure. To the right of the quarry is the Fat Man's Squeeze — a narrow passageway between two smooth pink giants. A yard or so on, a sharp right into the rock formations takes you two hundred feet to the top of the massive granite dome supporting the park's claim to fame. The precariously perched pink granite boulders do — albeit vaguely — resemble elephants. The largest — twenty-seven feet high, 680 tons — is named Dumbo. Scores of stonecutters carved their names in the dome's smooth surface, leaving a sober human trace in this otherwise extravagant abstraction.

Elephant Rock State Park

Those without sneakers may want to complete the path's circuit to the parking lot. Otherwise, walk around and below Dumbo into a Henry Moore brainscape. The trees growing tightly around a cluster of large boulders here conceal interconnecting rooms and narrow chasms open to the sky. Clambering pays off.

Back at the interpretive shelter, read about the process of erosion that formed the elephants, making them too soft for building materials — which is why they are still here today. Quarrying in the area was extensive. The attractive red granite was used in St. Louis at Laclede's Landing for paving, at Eads Bridge, and in a number of other buildings including City Hall.

Exit left. Take a moment to look at a second water-filled quarry a few yards beyond. Note the sculptural drilling marks on the smooth headwall.

Follow Missouri 21 north (left). At U look to your right: that is Buford Mountain, Missouri's second highest, set aside by the Nature Conservancy and open for hiking and nature study. A couple of miles north is Belleview, with attractive old buildings along the road.

Not all the Scotch-Irish who came to the region were mountaineers. At the end of the eighteenth century, Protestant farmers from Virginia, North Carolina and Tennessee began to settle in Bellevue Valley, still Spanish land. When Spanish-appointed officials sent a surveyor to measure out a creole claim in the valley, he was warned to keep his distance. This was part of what someone later dubbed "The Righteous Empire of Protestantism."

Unlike the mountaineers, these were work ethic Protestants. The spacious, ordered landscape around you, with its Shenandoah-style farmsteads, shows it.

Caledonia, a few miles north, likewise has a compact rational elegance very much in contrast with the surrounding Ozark insouciance. Missouri 21 is Caledonia's Main Street. Among several fine houses on the left is the frame Eversole House, whose facade is two-thirds of a normal Georgian one. Farther down, also on the left, are two classical revival brick houses, the first built in 1848 and the second in 1852. The latter succeeded in its attempt to outdo the former. Notice the tulip cutouts of its gazebo. Consider also Caledonia's urban manner: buildings right on the sidewalk, spaced fairly close together.

At Missouri 32 turn right. Turn right again at the first opportunity, the poorly marked College Street. On your right appears the 1872 Presbyterian Church, successor to the oldest Presbyterian church in the Mississippi, founded by Salmon Giddings in 1816. Its restrained design has neo-Gothic windows in a classical brick structure. To the east is a saltbox-shaped dwelling made up of two joined log structures. Note the different joints: on the left V-notches and on the right dovetail joints. Continue on College to Alexander. A right there will bring you back to Main — with a Methodist Church on the corner. Turn right on Main — and this time look right at the pressed tin storefronts.

Caledonia was home to congressman Willard Vandiver, who uttered the phrase, "I am from Missouri, you have got to show me."[5]

To return to St. Louis take Missouri 21 north to Missouri 47, which you may follow to Interstate 44. If you live in the city, however, you may prefer to take Missouri 21 all the way to St. Louis.

For information call:
Elephant Rocks State Park 1-697-5395
Fort Davidson State Historic Site 1-697-5395
Johnson's Shut-Ins State Park 1-546-2450
Union Electric Reservoir 1-365-9320

Queen's Canopy, Onondaga Cave State Park

Begins at exit 214, Interstate 44

The complexity of Missouri's cultural history is matched by the riches of its natural history. Elephant Rocks and Johnson's Shut-Ins state parks show how unusual that history is. But nowhere is the state's physical variety more evident than in the Meramec basin.

It is here that Missouri lives up to its old nickname, "the Cave State." The attractions of this area lie below as well as above ground; hence this chapter's name. Happily I-44 makes them all easily accessible from St. Louis; because of that, and because of their similarities, we are grouping them together. For a day trip, however, it may be better to plan on visiting only one or two of them.

We begin with the farthest, Onondaga Cave State Park, sixty-three miles southwest of Interstate 270. Get off I-44 at exit 214 and take H left toward Leasburg. It's almost seven miles to the interpretive center, where we now enter the cave.

Onondaga's first visitors, however, entered via the Lost River, the limpid, lifeless stream that flows through the cave, emptying a million gallons daily into the Meramec. The explorers' 1880s accounts of minerals here encouraged a mining company to purchase Onondaga for its cave onyx, used in architectural ornament of the day. Luckily the mining never began.

The cave was a popular attraction during the 1904 World's Fair. But only in the 1950s and 1960s, under the management of Lester B. Dill, nicknamed "America's Number One Caveman," was it widely publicized. The interpretive center displays a photo of Harpo Marx with Mr. Dill's business partner — who is dressed in a leopard skin. Mr. Dill, in a business suit, appears with Pearl Bailey.

Near the ticket desk is a map showing Missouri as the largest state of the Union. Here size is determined by each state's number of caves; using that standard, Missouri, with 4,500, truly is the biggest of them all.

How were they created? The shallow seas covering the Ozark region several hundred million years ago deposited layers of sedimentary rock. This became the Ozark plateau when the region was uplifted by a shift in the earth's crust. Rain created water-filled hollows in the now exposed soft rock. As streams and rivers eroded through the sedimentary layer, the hollows drained into these new valleys to become caves.

One of the visitor center's exhibits asks the question, "What grows but isn't alive?" When you and a guide enter the cave you get the answer: rock formations such as stalactites, stalagmites, and flowstones. This growth is slow. In the Big Room, the largest such space in Missouri — it's the size of a football field — is a pair of stalagmites called the Twins of the Cave. Despite their 450,000 years, they are of only modest height.

The world's largest active flowstone, the Queen's Canopy, is also included in the tour. The mining company who purchased the cave estimated that the Canopy was worth $1 million — but they could find no way to remove the Canopy without damaging it. Elsewhere in the cave is the equally impressive King's Canopy.

In the Lily Pad Room mineral-laden droplets falling into a pool of water have created lily pad forms. Close examination reveals these to be not unlike bathtub rings neglected for millenia.

The paths between these attractions are lined with formations of their own: icicles, string mops, handkerchiefs, pipe organs, bas relief trees, Gaudi columns, Alpine glaciers, and rood screens. All this was nearly lost, the guide notes: if 1970s' plans to dam the Meramec had come to fruition, almost the entire cave would have been submerged.

The Visitors' Center at Meramec State Park makes a similar point. Take I-44 northeast to its intersection with Missouri 185. Head south on Missouri 185 for three miles to the park entrance.

The uplifting of the Ozark plateau 250 million years ago was gradual, which meant that streams wandered sluggishly over the plateau. But as the lifting went on,

Lily Pad Room, Onondaga Cave State Park

the streams began to cut through the layers of rock, all the while maintaining their rambling courses. This created the beautifully named phenomenon of entrenched meanders.

That process, which continues, is the geological origin both of the Meramec's four-hundred-foot bluffs and of its wealth of natural habitats for flora and fauna.

The Visitors' Center shows the role flooding plays in maintaining this variety — a role vastly reduced when a river is dammed. The flood of a wild stream like the Meramec scours the bottom, redistributes sediment, and creates new banks and channels, thus producing habitats that permit a spectacular diversity of species.

Wildlife and wild rivers go together. But not all animals are content to leave well enough alone. Flooding — which has swollen the Meramec to as much as seventy-seven times its normal volume — disturbs those human beings who feel the need to control nature. In the late 1970s they almost succeeded in damming the Meramec; fortunately two out of three east-central Missourians voted to keep it natural.

Besides its excellent participatory exhibits, aquaria, and a wildlife viewing room, the Visitors' Center has a good twenty-minute slide show giving an idea of the park's offerings through the seasons.

The best way to enjoy the park is a walk along any of a number of trails through Meramec's 6,743 acres. They range from the half-mile Walking Fern Trail to the spectacular mile and a half Bluff View Trail to the six-mile Wilderness Trail. The center provides maps. Fishing and swimming are also possible. A handsome 1933 dining lodge, as well as overnight cabins and camping sites, make a longer stay inviting.

Meramec State Park, established in 1926, was the first of four state parks on the river. A number of county and

Jesse James Museum, Stanton

municipal parks added since then, as well as state lands and wildlife areas, have given substance to the idea of a Meramec River Greenway, a collection of ecologically coordinated open spaces all the way to the Mississippi. The public's increasing desire to work in harmony with nature has returned the valley to a wilder condition now than it has enjoyed since the turn of the century.

A few miles northeast on I-44 is exit 230, which takes you to an older tourist attraction, the Meramec Caverns. The name should sound familiar: it is emblazoned in garish colors on a thousand billboards in Missouri alone. Opened to the public in 1935 by Mr. Dill, the Caverns' aesthetic is of a pre-ecology era. Neon signs, colored light shows, and souvenirs all contribute to an experience where man is as much the actor as Mother Nature.

That doesn't mean that Jesse James' hideout in the cave is without interest or that the "Evolution of the Day" light show in the Submarine Garden doesn't have a modicum of crazy charm. No amount of corn can cover the beauty of these grand mineral formations. And who can resist a tour that underscores "America's Number One Cave Scene, the Stage and Stage Curtains of Meramec Caverns, or the Rock of Ages" not only with extravagant light effects, but also with Kate Smith singing "God Bless America." It's so shameless it's innocent.

When it rains, Meramec Caverns gets disappointed Six Flags customers. That's not a surprise. There's a relation here: if Meramec Caverns is a real environment with fake effects, Six Flags is a fake environment with real effects.

Travel northeast on I-44 to the Allenton Road exit. On your left Six Flags' roller coasters and its giant Ferris wheel "Colossus" make impressive sculptures against the hills.

Once you get close, however, sculpture gives way to

television. Six Flags bombards you with images. It uses St. Louis history — Soulard's Sweet Shop, Marquette's Market, and the Mine Train — as throw pillows, accents of color.

Foreign culture is decorative, too. King Arthur's Burgers Royale (Enter Ye Here), Merlin Guess-Your-Weight Game, Don Diego Jewelry and Tees, Chico's Toy Shop, Buenos Nachos, and La Cantina help reduce the world into consumable bits.

Amusement park rides transform danger into euphoria, as they have done for about four centuries. The first ride — a ice-covered wooden "hill" for sleds — was built in sixteenth-century Russia. Catherine the Great later had wheels put on the sled runners so that she could enjoy the ride in summer, too. Modern roller coasters and spinning octopi still provide a rush of fear while they last and a numb tranquility when they are over. Now, with one-price admission, there are no financial confrontations to interrupt the dizziness.

This is not to say that Six Flags doesn't deliver on its promise to amuse. On the contrary, the total benignity achieved by simplification of culture and removal of danger is entrancing. So entrancing, in fact, that most customers don't realize they are enjoying a crowded, urban environment, with all the chance contact with strangers and visual overload that most of them live in the suburbs trying to escape.

I-44 east takes you back to St. Louis.

For information call:
Meramec State Park 1-468-6072
Onondaga Cave 1-245-6600
Onondaga Cave State Park 1-245-6417
Six Flags 938-5300

The Museum of the Western Jesuit Missions, Florissant

Begins at North Hanley/Graham Road exit north,
Interstate 270

Cahokia, Altenburg, and the Barrens all suggest the
wealth of the St. Louis region's moral geography. This
tour confirms the role of religion in the land's development.

The first wave of missionary activity here began with
Pere Marquette's voyage in 1673. Not till the teens of the
nineteenth-century did a second wave come, largely a result of Bishop DuBourg's efforts. DuBourg, an enlight-
ened creole educator from Santo Domingo, was named
bishop of Louisiana and the Floridas in 1815. His new
diocese included the whole area of the Louisiana
Purchase, whose impoverished ecclesiastical condition
he knew well. At the time of his ordination in Rome, he
began an ambitious campaign to recruit help. As we shall
see, his endeavour to find men and women to minister to
his "truly desolate diocese" was crowned with success.

Philippine Duchesne, foundress of convents and
schools both in Florissant and St. Charles, as well as in
St. Louis itself, was one of the brightest figures in this
stellar second wave. Her virtues in fact led to her canoni-
zation in 1988, one of America's few saints.

Philippine had a tenacious affection for the old town
where this tour begins. "She loved Florissant with a kind
of vehemence," wrote her biographer.[1] Founded about
1785, in a luxuriant valley full of wild roses and berries,
whose rich loam was of an "inky blackness," Florissant

remained a beautiful village until recently. It began to change with the establishment of McDonnell-Douglas nearby; the village numbering in the hundreds in the 1930s, when French was still commonly spoken, now has a population of around 55,000.

Nonetheless its oldest section retains something of the character it had in Mother Duchesne's time. That is because she was not the only one to love it. Newer settlers continued to respect the old forms, as will be evident from a short drive around town, ending with her church and convent.

Head north from I-270 on Graham Road, which becomes St. Ferdinand after about a mile. Soon thereafter turn right on Harrison. At 410, just across rue St. Jean, is an 1840 white brick house with an elaborate cornice. Turn left on rue St. Jean for the half-hidden 1836 Bellisime House at 359, also brick. Its single story with attic and dormer windows, along with its gallery porches, give it a typically creole form.

In these two houses you have Florissant's nineteenth-century ethnic history: the original French and French Canadian settlers were joined, toward the middle of that century, by German Catholics. French forms were often retained, but with an infusion of German materials and tastes.

A right on Washington and a left on rue St. Jacques leads to the 1842 Baptiste Aubuchon House at 450, which often displays a fleur-de-lis flag. Continue on St. Jacques two blocks to rue St. Francois where a right takes you downtown. Look for the woodsy Victorian Union Church, this Catholic town's oldest Protestant church.

Continue on St. Francois past the new but traditionally styled City Hall on the left. Turn left just after onto Brown. At the southeast corner of Brown and rue St. Louis is the 1800 Aubuchon House, a pristine creole construction. Grooved weatherboarding covers its upright logs.

Follow Brown to rue St. Denis, where you turn left. Notice how the scale of the houses and the lack of sidewalks help preserve the old town's atmosphere. On the northeast corner with Jefferson is the 1850 Archambault House, red brick with Federal details. Across Jefferson is the 1873 Hendel's Market. The warmth of the old brick, the spires of the church, and the harmonious scale of the other buildings make this a felicitous townscape.

Turn left on Jefferson. The impressive complex of the Sacred Heart Church and School was built for a German parish established in 1866; its name is an homage to St. Philippine's French-based order. The Herz Jesu Schule, closest to the corner, was built in 1889. Next is the 1893 church, with finely detailed cornice and belltower. Turn right on rue St. Louis and look at the rectory's chimneys: even though it's a German building, the iron tie-rods are secured with fleur-de-lis.

Continue on rue St. Louis to 406, a taupe frame house with simple details and a well-proportioned Ionic porch. Farther down at 306 is the black and white 1857 Home Place, whose sign informs us that its builder was a French riverboat plyman.

Turn right on rue St. Pierre. At the end of the block, across rue St. Denis, is the moody Casa Alvarez, built in 1790 for the royal Spanish military storekeeper.

Turn left on St. Denis and left on St. Ferdinand. Looking across the Spanish Land Grant Park, where the colonial town's militia used to drill, you see the steeple of St. Ferdinand's. A right on St. Francois takes you across Fountain Creek to this church, the oldest one in America dedicated to the Sacred Heart. Along with the convent it is open from April to mid-December.

The cornerstone, a gift of Mother Duchesne, was laid

St. Ferdinand's

in 1821 (despite the date in the lunette over the door); legend has it that Philippine inscribed it with the statement, "My heart will abide here." The church, consecrated by Bishop Rosati in 1832, was extended and given a new facade in 1870.

Philippine and four companions brought the Society of the Sacred Heart to the United States in 1818. After a disappointing year in St. Charles the nuns moved here, where Mother Duchesne was to spend fourteen of her next thirty-three years. By the fall of 1820 the two and a half story brick convent, to the right of the church, was complete.

The convent did not always thrive, but the energetic saint kept it open. Finally, in 1847, convent and school were taken over by the Sisters of Loretto, who remained till just after World War I. (They relocated in Webster Groves, founding what is now Webster University.)

The interior is well worth a visit for its engaging simplicity, and above all for a look at the cubbyhole under the stairs near the chapel. Here Philippine insisted on sleeping into her late 60s, when her superior sent her to a room upstairs. This self-denial, her way of following Christ, was in sharp opposition to what she saw around her "in this country, . . . luxury and soft living . . . indulged in to a disgusting excess."[2]

Father Peter De Smet, who appears later in this tour, was ordained in this church. He was another brilliant recruit of Bishop DuBourg, relics of whose patron, St. Valentine, are enclosed in the wax figure under the main altar.

Outside, the picturesque complex is overwhelmed by asphalt, a characteristic of too many Catholic institutions in Missouri. The attractive structure with a wooden bell tower was a school.

Backtrack across the creek and turn right on St. Charles, where you will see, before the end of the street, two tiny green and white frame houses. Turn right on Washington, which becomes Charbonier after Lindbergh.

Almost a mile and a half beyond Lindbergh turn left on Howdershell Road. Half a mile farther watch for the St. Stanislaus Jesuit Historical Museum sign on the left. Follow the driveway all the way back to the front of the complex.

In 1823 a group of Flemish Jesuits arrived in Florissant. They too were responding to Bishop DuBourg's call. He intended to start a school for Indian boys, where the latter would learn the white man's ways and the former would learn Indian manners and languages.

But relations between Jesuits and scholars were trying. The boys' natural reaction to European discipline and especially to manual labor — squaw work — was flight, provoking more than one early morning chase. After seven years' struggle with a mere thirty charges, the fathers closed the school.

If the boys did not learn a great deal, the Jesuits did; it was here that Peter De Smet first gained the understanding of the Indians that would make him their beloved "Black Robe," the very model of the good white man.

The novitiate of St. Stanislaus, established after the Indian school's demise, was to become, by the time of its closing in 1971, the oldest Jesuit novitiate in the world. The cupola-topped central limestone portion, built in 1840-49, now houses a museum.

The museum and Mother Duchesne's convents hold memorabilia as important to an understanding of St. Louis' history as anything in the region. Unfortunately they do not receive funding to match this importance; St. Stanislaus especially merits more attention.

Yet even in its present state the collection of Indian and missionary mementos is both instructive and fascinating. On the first floor, for instance, we see Father De Smet's Sioux deerskin coat, his traveling pyx and crucifix, as well as his cigar box and wine flask kit. These were well-used; he traveled more than a quarter of a million miles alternately seeking souls and support for his missions.

Inside the chapel, to the right, is a small carved wooden tabernacle door from Paraguay, whose Jesuit Indian protectorate De Smet hoped to emulate in the United States.

The European atmosphere of these rooms owes as much to the good paintings noble benefactors sent across the Atlantic as to the Jesuits' own continental background.

The second floor features a Kansas Mission Room, with a compact walnut altar. The library on this floor, the classroom on the third, and the bedrooms on both, give an idea of life in the seminary. A room displaying books written by St. Stanislaus alumni is yet another indication of the far-ranging influence of this institution.

The view southward from the windows upstairs, or from the entrance below, shows the ghostly remnant of a formal garden, once center of a vast property. St. Stanislaus grew grapes for Missouri's first winery, which, since it produced altar wine, was the only one to remain open through Prohibition.

The suburbs — which have nearly overwhelmed the eighteenth-century creole villages on this tour — are visibly encroaching on St. Stanislaus. Gateway College of Evangelism now occupies most of the seminary's later buildings.

On your way back to Howdershell, turn left into the parking lot behind the complex. The orderly matrix of white tombstones before you is the Jesuit cemetery. De Smet's grave is in the third row near the left edge.

Turn left onto Howdershell which becomes James S. McDonnell Boulevard and crosses over I-270. Go left on Fee Fee Road past a thick oak which has survived the area's transformation from wilderness to high tech. You arrive shortly at the corner of Fee Fee Road and Fee Fee Hills Road, both named for Nicolas Beaugenou whose nickname — all creoles had one — was Fi-Fi, pronounced Fee-Fee. Here is the handsome brick mid-nineteenth-century St. Cin farmhouse with a view of the fields beyond Pershall Park — and I-270 beyond that.

Jog right then left with Fee Fee Road. A couple of blocks left on Utz Lane, at 615, is the mid-1820s' Utz-Tesson House, an engulfed farmstead. A U-turn on Utz Lane brings you to Lindbergh opposite the Ford Motor Plant.

Turn right, and right again at James S. McDonnell Boulevard. Note the dashing red, yellow and blue details of McDonnell Douglas' HOK-designed building on the corner. At this writing it is possible to turn into the driveway and head to the Lindbergh facade for a better view.

Back on McDonnell Boulevard, make a left on Fee Fee Road. This woodsy stretch is likely to disappear under an expanded Lambert Field. Jog left on Missouri Bottom Road whose name and landscape suggest Bridgeton's French name, Marais des Liards — Cottonwood Swamp. Marais des Liards was mentioned by the Spanish lieutenant governor in 1798, who noted that all its young men were hunters.

Pick up Fee Fee to the right. Cross Natural Bridge. The 1870 Payne-Gentry House appears a half mile to the right, nestled in a recreational park.

Another half mile brings you to St. Charles Rock Road. Immediately to the left stands the 1869 Mizpah Presbyterian Church. Across the road on the left stands Fee Fee Baptist Church, established in 1807 by Missouri's first permanent Baptist minister, Thomas R. Musick. The oldest part of the present complex was completed in 1870, while its 1829 predecessor remains on the original site at the corner of Fee Fee and Old St. Charles Rock Roads, half a mile south.

A right on St. Charles Rock Road currently takes you five miles to a slender eighty-six-year-old bridge. At the end of it, turn right on Second. Looking left you will see the red brick Sacred Heart Academy, with its octagonal chapel in the garden. To get there turn left on Decatur then left again on Fourth. Follow the arrows for the St. Philippine Duchesne Shrine.

In the eighteenth- and early-nineteenth centuries, this new land was settled by extremely well-suited (which means half-savage) frontiersmen, and apparently unsuited and remarkably civilized people like Philippine Duchesne.

She and St. Charles were born the same year, 1769. But

Philippine matured more gracefully, for the village's character long reflected that of its rough backwoodsman founder, Louis Blanchette *dit* Le Chasseur, and his Pawnee wife Angelique.

Philippine's enterprising but close-knit family was distinguished in her native Grenoble both in business and in public affairs. Her desire for missionary work began early, when, at eight or ten years old, she heard Jesuit accounts of the Indians. This desire was not to be satisfied for decades, partly because religion and especially conventual life was scorned in the revolutionary France she came to age in.

She was able, however, to become a nun. Her piety was so strong that she would pray whole nights through, kneeling upright, unsupported, in the convent chapel.

When Bishop DuBourg made an appeal to the Sacred Heart order for teachers for his huge but needy American diocese, Philippine's prayers were answered. At age forty-nine she headed for the wilds of Missouri.

As happened with many who preceded and were to follow her across the Atlantic, her hope fed on misinformation. . . "The land is so fertile where we shall live that the cattle are entirely hidden in the prairie grass."

On arrival in New Orleans, she and her four companions were to travel upstream on one of the earliest Mississippi steamboats, "a wonderful invention." America impressed her. True, "in this country there are no revenues set aside for ecclesiastics," and "the inhabitants build quickly but not solidly," eat "bear grease, which is disgusting," and place beds next to open windows: "out here . . . no one pays any attention to drafts." But she was convinced that Americans "will not be satisfied with mediocrity," and that they "are deeper in character than the creoles," who were "softer, lighter, and more pleasure-loving."

One Creole in particular disappointed her. Bishop DuBourg ordered her to establish the convent not in lively

St. Louis, but in St. Charles. "St. Charles seemed to me a tomb in which our enterprise . . . would be buried," she wrote to the head of the Society of the Sacred Heart in France.

Later, somewhat more optimistic, she wrote that Americans were "constantly pouring into this section of the country — restless people, who hope St. Charles will become a great commercial link between the United States and China, for the Upper Missouri rises not far from another river that pours its water into the Pacific Ocean at a place where the crossing to Asia takes just two weeks." But this foreshortened geography of the Northwest Passage had a downside. "Hence," she added, "everything is very scarce and very expensive here." And despite its future dominance of the China trade, St. Charles seemed "the remotest village in the United States."

The worst of it was that she never even saw real Indians, "because the Americans from the East are pushing them out." The settlers' racism aroused her ire. "The most marked characteristic of the Americans is scorn for anyone and anything that is not American." These prejudiced settlers "are as ignorant of morality as the Indians are."

There were compensations. "We dig in the garden . . . water the cow, clean out her little stable — the only one in this place, for all the animals wander at large." Later they got another cow. "People told us these cows would be frenzied if we tethered them in our grounds, but they are behaving nicely and follow us around like two big dogs; they even try to follow us into the house."

Would the nuns ever be able to domesticate the Americans as they had their cows? She came to realize that the frontiersmen had the same needs as the Indians. But evangelization seemed impossible. "Every household has its drunkards. The girls are crazy about dancing . . . It takes saints to work on hearts so poorly prepared."

Philippine despaired. "The soul is utterly alone here." But she knew that "the truest crosses are those we do not choose ourselves . . . Perhaps He wants His missionary nuns to sanctify themselves on failure."

After an unsuccessful year in St. Charles they left for Florissant, Philippine delaying a day because the cows didn't want to walk in the sun. The next morning, "with cabbages to appease the cows," she wrote, "I perched on top of a cart, dividing my attention between my relics and the chickens."

But, she later observed, "nothing under heaven is stable in the section of the world in which we live." Not even failure. Mother Duchesne's St. Charles school did succeed in time, and once heathen St. Charles came to know real religious fervor.

Philippine's personal ambition succeeded too; in 1841 she was able to go to the Potawatami Indian mission in what is now Kansas. Five hundred braves on horseback came out to celebrate her arrival, circling round the wagon, shooting guns in the air and performing riding tricks. She had waited a lifetime for this.

Her age — she had begun her eighth decade — and infirmity kept her from much activity there. But she was able to do what she liked and did best; in fact the Potawatomi's called her "Woman-Who-Prays-Always." They must have felt her devotion to them, for they made her frequent gifts of wild plums, eggs, or fresh straw for her bed.

The austerity of the shrine's unfinished interior might have pleased Mother Duchesne, who is buried here. Above her sarcophagus hangs a crucifix from the Grenoble convent she entered as a young woman. A St. Louisan purchased it for his own chapel; when he learned of its relation to the saint he donated it to the nuns. Look at the foot warmer and much mended chair in a glass covered niche to the left. A native of the south of France, Mother Duchesne suffered from Missouri winters, yet even in her old age she considered resting her feet on the ember-filled tin box an unconscionable luxury. She repaired the hide seat of the chair herself.

Guides will take you to the original 1835 convent, hidden on three sides by later additions. In the tiny room where Mother Duchesne died are objects she was fond of: a painting on wood of the Adoration of the Magi, a Madonna, her writing desk.

The most moving bit of memorabilia is perhaps the most inconsequential. In a cabinet sits a suite of doll furniture the elderly Mother Duchesne elaborately embroidered for a sick student — typical of her efforts to bring grace to the lives around her.

Exit left on Clark. Cross Second and curve right onto Riverside Drive which takes you past the 1892 MKT Depot. At the end of Riverside, curve right, then right on Main Street. Here, to the right, is St. Charles' oldest building, the 1789 Blanchette Chouteau Mill. In the 1820s it was the westernmost grist mill in the United States; wagon trains stopped here for provisions. Next door is the Old Mill Stream Inn restaurant, with a pleasant garden next to the stream itself.

It's hard to get a sense of what St. Charles must have been like in its post-Lewis-and-Clark heyday when, as the WPA guide to Missouri puts it, "the dust of the town streets never settled."[3] The last outpost of civilization for American pioneers, Gold Rushers, and German immigrants now purveys potpourri, candles, and greeting cards to tourists.

Continue down Main. At 719 South Main is the 1790 French Duplex. At 301 South Main, built in 1799, a mob attacked Elijah Lovejoy after one of his rousing antislavery speeches in 1837. A mob in Alton killed him a month later.

Cross First Capitol Drive. On the right is the Tourism Center and then the First State Capitol Historic Site where Missouri's legislature met for its first five years. An interpretive center stands next door.

The official tone established here with period antiques and crisp tours is a nice overlay on what is a spicy, robust story. Missouri's first legislature bore out the adage that politics makes strange bedfellows: cultivated Creoles mixed with illiterate backwoodsmen in what must have been interesting discussion. One described himself as "a tearin critter of the catamount school . . . there is few who can beat me swapping horses or guessing at the weight of a bar [bear]. I have come here because my people voted for me, knowing I was an honest man and could make as good whiskey and apple brandy at my still as any man."[4]

Turn left on Jefferson for the 1901 Courthouse. On the corner of Jefferson and Second is a granite stone marking Boone's Lick Trail, the great point of departure for settlers heading west. From it branched the Salt Lake, the Oregon, and the Santa Fe Trails.

Continue up the hill on Jefferson where a collection of pretty houses faces a parking garage. Turn right on Fifth. A few blocks beyond turn right on Morgan and left on Second, which will take you through St. Charles' antique-filled Frenchtown district.

Follow the signs for Missouri 94 which runs east into a rich alluvial plain. Here the Indian tribes whose sons studied with Florissant's Jesuits bivouacked. About ten miles beyond St. Charles you pass near the Marais Temps Clair Wildlife Area; this swampy lowland is a remnant of the former course of the Missouri river. The Missouri floods this narrow peninsula often enough, charging across to the Mississippi.

A few miles farther turn left on J for Portage des Sioux. The town was named for a legendary group of Indians who took advantage of this narrow bridge between the Missouri and the Mississippi. Pursued down the Missouri by Osages whose village they had just raided, the Sioux evaded their enemies by carrying their canoes two miles across land to the Mississippi. The Osages continued paddling down the Missouri, mystified by the Sioux's disappearance.

Portage, founded in the late-eighteenth century, was granted common fields by the king of Spain. It is the only town in Missouri which has never sold off its holdings; farmers lease the fields for twenty years at a time.

The town was an important base against England's Indian allies in the War of 1812; at the end of the war peace treaties were signed here with representatives from nineteen tribes. Peaceful Portage is now an important base for weekend boaters.

At the end of J, turn right then quickly left on Farnham. Just after the 1879 Church of St. Francis of Assisi, turn right on Second. A few blocks beyond turn left on Le Sieur for the shrine of Our Lady of the River.

The twenty-seven-foot Madonna you see here was erected to thank the Virgin for saving the town from a 1951 flood. Walk out along the pier where plaques outline the town's history. Spectacular views of bluff and river, especially at sunset, will perhaps attract your attention more than the fiberglass statue and its yellow neon halo.

Backtrack to Missouri 94. You may turn left and return to St. Louis via U.S. 67. Or you may backtrack to St. Charles and return on Interstate 70.

For information call:
First State Capitol Historical Site 946-9282
St. Charles Convention and Visitors Bureau 946-7776
St. Philippine Duchesne Shrine 946-6127
The Museum of the Western Jesuit Missions 837-3525

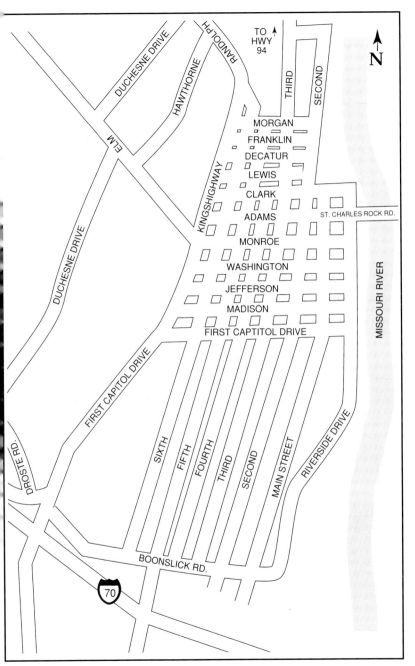

ST. CHARLES

1833 church, Femme Osage

Begins at U.S. 40/Interstate 64 and Missouri 94

Two great waves of immigration, the first Anglo-American, the second German, followed the French into the St. Louis region. Each had a magnetic leader. Daniel Boone led Americans here even before the territory was American. A generation later, Gottfried Duden lured Germans to what was still mostly a wilderness. Their followers settled on the northern bank of the Missouri River, which this tour parallels.

Few men have lived the American ideal so intensely as Daniel Boone. His genius for the ways of the wilderness, matched by his thoroughgoing love of freedom, made him a myth in his own time. The geographical consequences of his career have proven the myth's substance ever since. He blazed a trail into Kentucky that thousands followed, making him the father of that state. He played a similar role, though less dramatically, in the development of Missouri. In fact he ended his days here, having spent almost exactly as much time in this territory as in Kentucky.

Just west of Missouri 94's intersection with U.S. 40/I-64 is the August A. Busch Wildlife Area. Along with the Weldon Spring and Howell Island Wildlife Areas, it forms a 17,000-acre expanse of country still almost as empty as Boone found it. Now as then it affords rich hunting, fishing, and flora- and fauna-watching opportunities. The Busch Wildlife Area headquarters, to the right on D, distributes information and maps, including one of a 7.7-mile auto tour.

The Weldon Spring Ordnance Works, westward on Missouri 94, suggests that however untouched nature may appear hereabouts, it is far from virgin. This army munitions plant produced TNT during World War II and uranium later; radioactive waste was stored in a nearby quarry and in lagoons behind the plant.

Continue on Missouri 94 to Defiance, a village of pleasant white frame buildings. Near the west end of town are two taverns whose names hint at the domesticity prevailing hereabouts: one is Terry and Betty's, the other Bob and Shirley's. Turn right on Defiance Road to the 1906 St. Paul's Evangelische Kirche; here turn around, backtrack to Second Street and turn left. Take the first right past a handsome 1840s' brick house and the appropriately named Pleasant Hill Methodist Church, where another right will bring you back to Missouri 94. Backtrack east on it a mile to F.

Left on F, which will lead to what is widely — and wrongly — advertised as "America's Most Historic Gem, The Daniel Boone Home." This fine dwelling is historic — if not quite our "most historic." The blue limestone structure belonged not to Daniel, however, but to Nathan, his youngest son.

This is not hairsplitting. Daniel Boone's whole story might be summarized as a refusal of the ties that bind, of home. "They acquire no attachment to Place," wrote Lord Dunmore of the Americans. "But wandering about Seems engrafted in their Nature; and it is a weakness incident to it that they Should for ever immagine the Lands further off are Still better than those upon which they are already settled." Dunmore, royal governor of Virginia, had sent Boone into Kentucky; he seems to have written his description with the great frontiersman in mind.[1]

Boone's descendants shared this "Nature." In 1795 his son Daniel Morgan visited the Spanish territory beyond the Mississippi. Empty and vast, it pleased him greatly. Lieutenant Governor Trudeau, who wanted settlers, assured young Boone that the Spanish would reward the emigration of his legendary father with grants of land for himself and for all those he brought along.

But Daniel senior hesitated. Kentucky had long seemed so desirable a place that one preacher, to describe the joys of the afterlife, told his congregation, "O my dear honeys, heaven is a Kentucky of a place."[2] But by 1799, with his debts mounting and his lands all taken from him, Boone decided to leave. He chopped down a giant yellow poplar, hewed a sixty-foot pirogue, and set

The Daniel Boone House

out for the long voyage down the Ohio and up the Mississippi. He was sixty-five.

St. Louis gave him a hero's welcome, with flourishes and fanfares and rifles cracking in salute. A grant of close to nine thousand acres followed, Boone's prize for the scores of Kentucky families he attracted to the population-hungry territory.

But the old backwoodsman was nonchalant about his property, neither clearing it nor building a house. Perhaps he was too busy hunting or fulfilling his judicial duties as syndic of the Femme Osage region. As a result, after the Louisiana Purchase, American officials refused to recognize his right to the grant.

It did not seem to disturb him very much. Boone knew how to live on the land lightly, like the Indians. This relative freedom from property ideas was in harmony with his disregard for other conventional restraints. When the War of 1812 broke out he at once volunteered. But the government considered seventy-eight years too many for a soldier.

Boone's age didn't keep him from other ventures. He continued his long hunts "into the remotest wilderness he can reach . . ." well beyond his eightieth year.[3] He was as free of the constraint of resentment as he was of ideas about age. The plenteous game caught in these expeditions went to pay the last of his Kentucky creditors, whose claims he honored even when doubtful.

Boone died here in 1820, in his eighty-sixth year, not an unhappy man. As his excellent biographer put it, "He had seen the land when it was new and it gladdened him as riches never could."[4]

The house is worth the half-hour tour. Finely styled within as without, it has many Boone family mementos, including two beautifully carved wooden mantels, said to be the work of Daniel himself, and a 1791 powder horn on which Boone etched his name and a primitive horse and saddle. There is also a wealth of seventeenth-, eighteenth-, and nineteenth-century furniture here.

Boone's likeness in the room where he and Rebecca slept calls to mind an anecdote showing his amused awareness of his mythical stature. A painter, who came to him in his last years to do a portrait, asked if in his wanderings he had ever been lost. "No, I can't say as ever I was lost," came the reply. "But I was once bewildered for three days."[5]

Rebecca bore Daniel ten children — fewer than the average frontier family had. She died in 1813 after fifty-six years of marriage. In the ground floor kitchen are many spinning, weaving, and cooking tools. The cosy appeal of the rooms here should not blind us to the hard lot of pioneer women. One pioneer wife remarked that the frontier was fine for the men and the dogs but hell on the women. Few lived to Rebecca Boone's old age.

"The Daniel Boone Home Is A True Excursion Into History!" its boosters brag. However applicable to the house, the claim cannot be made of the "historic" village of transplanted old buildings at the back of the Nathan Boone dwelling.

It is ironic that anyone should want to clutter this view, the last one enjoyed by a great man who loathed being crowded. It is even more ironic that we are supposed to be grateful for it. However authentic the single structures may be, collectively the "village" is false. Yet if it weren't for such theme parks and parklets, we would perhaps lose even more of the buildings that remind us of our heritage. The pseudo-village goes with the "Most Historic Gem" aspect of this experience.

Turn left as you exit the Boone Home lot. About a mile and a half down the road, along which you may see a number of log buildings and a handsomely recycled

stone barn, turn left across a one-lane bridge onto
Femme Osage Road. After passing several beautiful
farmsteads, the road winds its way to a stop sign. Turn
left. Soon you'll come on Femme Osage.

Femme Osage, with its buildings turned toward the
visitor in greeting, is a village that looks happy to be just
where it is, nestled along a creek in this remote valley.
But its sense of place owes as much to its nineteenth-
century German inhabitants as to its site. Unlike their
American contemporaries, they had a strong attachment
to home. It's pleasant to stroll up to the cemetery, enjoying the clean-lined church, with its spirited green Gothic
shutters and its ogival back door.

The road through the town will take you to a T intersection; turn left. At Missouri 94 turn left for Augusta,
another deep-rooted German community. Take the *second* right, Church Street, so named for the surprisingly
pink brick church there. Church Street ends at Hackmann. On the left-hand corner is the Harmonieverein
Halle and behind it a gingerbread bandstand. This music society was founded in 1856 "to cheer up life through
vocal and instrumental music as well as by promoting
social intercourse through friendship and congeniality."[6]

Turn right on Hackmann, then left on Lower. On the
first street to the right, Locust, is the Augusta Antiqua
and Country Store Museum, a turn-of-the-century country store open on warm weather weekends. Continue
one more block on Lower to Walnut Street. Turn right.
Catercorner from the Ebenezer United Church of Christ
is a white Victorian Gothic house richly endowed with
glass-globed lightning rods.

Among Walnut's fine Victorian structures, note especially the tin-roofed mid-nineteenth-century brick house
next to the well-stocked Augusta Emporium. Make a
left on Jackson and a left on Chestnut. At Washington

Street, turn right. Go to Main Street, turn right again, then left down Publick to what used to be Water Street.

This is the oldest part of Augusta, as the dilapidated state of the onetime hotel here suggests. The town's site was chosen in 1836 by Leonard Harold, a follower of Daniel Boone, for its fine river landing. By mid-century Augusta had become a commercial and cultural center for the German settlers who predominated in this region. But the Missouri River, not always faithful to its bed, flooded its way into a channel across the valley after a particularly deep freeze in the winter of 1872. The original quarter, like the landing itself, has all but disappeared. Perhaps the conversion of the old railroad right of way into the Katy Trail for hikers and bikers will bring life back to this neighborhood.

Fortunately the community had resources other than the errant river. The countryside around prospered with grain, livestock, and especially vineyards. There were thirteen wineries here before Prohibition. Go back to Main Street and turn left. Turn right on Webster Street, then left on Augusta Bottom for Mount Pleasant Winery.

First established in 1881, this winery was revived in the 1960s by Lucian Dressel, a dairy farmer from Granite City. He replanted the vineyards with stock from St. Stanislaus Seminary in Florissant, along with several European varieties. Mount Pleasant's successful vintage port is made using techniques learned from St. Stanislaus' Jesuits.

A complimentary tour takes you by the modern stainless steel French and Italian wine pressing equipment and through two original cellars. Here the wine is aged in casks made of Yugoslavian, American and French oaks or of cypress, each of which instills a different character. The barrels themselves are made by coopers in Hannibal.

From the lawn next to the Cheese Wedge (which

offers provisions for a picnic lunch) you can see why the town was first named Mount Pleasant. The view is majestic both in summer, when the vast bottomland is lush with corn, and in winter, when it is black and dramatic.

Take Augusta Bottom back to Jackson and turn left. If you haven't picnicked at Mount Pleasant, consider the Cookie Jar, which offers a decent sourdough sandwich. More food, especially produce in season, and cider, is purveyed at Centennial Farm, farther down Jackson toward Missouri 94.

Turn left on Missouri 94 for Dutzow. Here lived the man who attracted at least as many thousands to Missouri as Daniel Boone. But while Boone's westward moves seemed almost instinctive, "engrafted in [his] Nature," as Lord Dunmore put it, Gottfried Duden, a German jurist, came to Missouri to conduct an experiment.

After studying his country's poverty, overcrowding, and political repression, Duden concluded that emigration was the common German's only solution. But before recommending it he wanted a first-hand experience of frontier life. That desire brought him, late in 1824, to Missouri.

He was soon starry-eyed: ". . . the entire life of the inhabitants of these regions seemed like a dream to me at first . . . ." Even after time had passed he confessed wilderness existence was "almost a fantasy when I consider what nature has to offer man here . . . . The hills and valleys are all covered with forests, but in such groupings that it appears as if an artist had laid out a park . . . . One can travel hundreds of miles between gigantic tree trunks without a single ray of sunlight falling upon one's head. The soil is so black here from the plant mold that has been accumulating since primeval days that one seems to be walking on a coal bed."[7]

Duden believed that the soil was in fact too rich to

grow wheat; a few years of vegetable growing would have to deplete it first. Even then it would not need fertilizer for the first century.[8] Without any cultivation the hillsides were covered with grapes, pecan trees whose nuts were plenteous and tasty, and pawpaws whose fruits were "hard to distinguish from a well-prepared sweet custard."[9]

His own life was as idyllic as the land.

> My daily routine is as follows: At sunrise I go outdoors, usually with a fowling piece. I roam around for about an hour, shoot partridges, doves, or squirrels, and also turkeys . . . and return to eat my breakfast. After breakfast I read . . . I then occupy myself, as calmly as I ever did in Germany, with the sciences. Shortly before noon I stop, walk in the garden, or go to the spring. After the meal I mount my horse either to visit my neighbors or to enjoy the beauty of nature in the forests, on the hills, or in the valley.[10]

The backbreaking toil most pioneers suffered finds little place in Duden's account. That may be because Duden, a rich man, hired a cook and a field hand. A nearby farmer delivered turkeys every week, since Duden himself wasn't a good shot. His easy situation explains some of the enthusiasm of his *Report on a Journey to the Western States of North America*, which he published in Germany in 1833. But it doesn't explain why the book become a deeply influential best-seller.

Perhaps that was a natural response to Duden's painting of Missouri as a paradise where men could build the life of their choice. This vision touched two hopes always resonating in European thought about America. One had to do with a land where ideals might be fulfilled. The other had to do with a land where men might be fulfilled.

Both hopes were Utopian, but the latter appealed to practical-minded types. Duden paid attention even to the minutiae of what immigrants might expect, cataloging everything from corn whiskey, "as good as the best French brandy," and shop girls more polite than any in Germany, to mosquitoes, ticks, fleas, snakes, possums, parrots, vultures, corn stealing squirrels, and skunks. His combination of apparent practicality and romantic idealism brought the Germans in droves. A contemporary German writer remarked that between 1841 and 1846 nineteen thousand had left Bremen *alone* for the States. Among those coming to Missouri thanks to Duden's influence were Altenburg's Martin Stephan and the Hanoverians of Washington.

Duden's vision, meant to stimulate emigration of the lower orders, was in fact especially effective with aristocrats, artists and intellectuals, often as unfit for frontier rigors as Duden himself. Because their education often equaled their impracticality, they got the ironic nickname of Latin Farmers.

Though ignorant of frontier life, they were well acquainted with the good life. One of Dutzow's founder's chief concerns was the establishment of a club. Baron Wilhelm Johann von Bock, before building a stable or barn, or even a house, constructed a clubhouse with a billiard table, games, and a small library. He and some of his peers hired their American "peasant" neighbors to do the work to leave them free to pass their time there.

Despite unrealistic expectations and pretensions, some of these Latin Farmers — or their sons — did succeed. Baron von Spankeren, for example, ran a tannery and loan office near the town. Another von Bock surveyed most of Kansas. Some however found themselves hopelessly in debt to the farmers they'd hired. Driven to a choice between menial labor in St. Louis and death, the least suited at times chose the latter: a number of suicides are recorded.

Turn right with Missouri 94 just outside Dutzow.

After a mile and half turn right on poorly marked Boone Monument Road. You'll pass a classic nineteenth-century red brick farmhouse with a small white porch and a cluster of much-used outbuildings. Now the Stemme farm, this was the home of David Bryan, nephew of Daniel and Rebecca Boone. West of the farmhouse is a white sign directing you up a few stairs to the graveyard.

Boone descendants have erected a bronze and granite marker here for Rebecca and Daniel. Kentucky also claims to have the Boone graves within its borders; they exhumed Rebecca and the body beside hers in 1845 and reinterred them in Frankfort. But it seems that Daniel had been buried at Rebecca's feet; Kentucky took possession of one of the many black Missourians who shared this graveyard. At the western edge of the plot, almost falling down the hill, is the grave of Tildy, a beloved mammy.

Return to Missouri 94 and follow it west seven miles to Treloar. Follow N to the edge of the hamlet. Turn left at the corner of N and the town's main street and notice the zippy tin facade of the bank and adjoining brick store. Turn right just after for the green and white tile acade next to the country club. At the end of the street turn right and continue straight on N.

N takes you north a mile to Holstein. After a sharp curve, look to the left for a picturesque building with cupola and tin roof. Soon after appears Holstein's "downtown," at whose center, N and Mill Road, is the abandoned General Store with a tin facade. Holstein also has three graveyards and an 1884 red brick German church.

Continue on N, which joins Missouri 47. Turn left for Warrenton, eight and a half miles north.

At Boone's Lick Road and Missouri 47 there is a stoplight. Turn left. Boone's Lick Road (Main Street in Warrenton) led to the Howard County salt springs Daniel Boone discovered on one of his long expeditions into unknown territory. With his sons Nathan and Daniel Morgan he was soon producing thirty bushels of salt a day, which they sealed in hollowed logs and floated downriver to market. The trail leading to Boone's Lick was to become one of the principal pioneer routes, the last of the roads west Daniel Boone opened.

Head down intact Main Street to the Classical Revival courthouse built in 1869. Go left a block beyond on South Morgan and left again on Walton. At 206 note the Victorian Gothic cottage with a turret over its porch. Behind the courthouse is the Warren County Museum.

Farther up Walton at 102 and 103 are brick Victorian houses. Continue to Missouri 47. Turn left. At the light turn right on M (once again Boone's Lick Road). Follow M nine miles to OO and turn left. After a mile and a half, OO becomes N. Along the way watch for lushly pastured horse farms and a nineteenth-century dwelling or two.

N connects with U.S. 40. Take U.S. 40/I-64 east to St. Louis.

If you want a speedy rather than scenic return, Missouri 47 will take you north to Interstate 70.

For information call:
August A. Busch Memorial Wildlife Area 441-4554
Howell Island Wildlife Area 441-4554
Daniel Boone House 1-987-2221
Mount Pleasant Vineyards and Winery 1-228-4419
Warren County Museum 1-456-3820
Weldon Spring Wildlife Area 441-4554

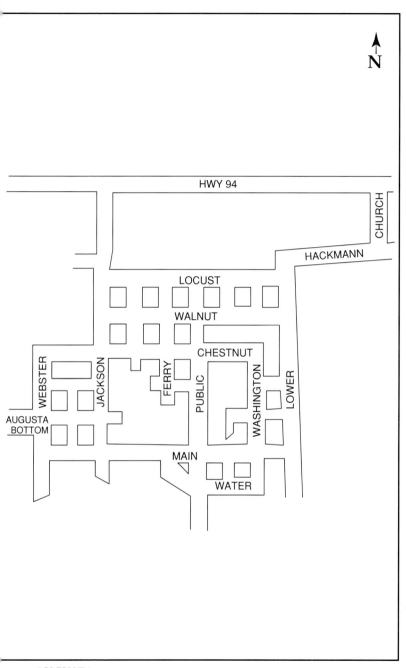

AUGUSTA

Gasconade County Courthouse

Begins at Missouri 94 and 19

We usually think of nineteenth-century America as the
place where people came in search of a new life. But sometimes what impelled men and women to cross the seas
was a hope of saving their old life. Many German emigrants
did not want Eden; they wanted to escape the feeling of
rootlessness brought on by religious and political changes
in Europe. Duden's Latin Farmers and the Saxon Lutherans
acted on this motive. So — and most successfully — did
the settlers of Hermann.

Hermann was created by Germans whose goal was to
conserve their old ways. Having moved first to
Philadelphia, they were distressed at the Americanization
of their children. How could they protect their culture?
They decided to go west, where they might found a town
German in every particular. In 1836 they organized the
German Settlement Society of Philadelphia, which sent
scouts to Texas, Minnesota, Wisconsin, Illinois, Indiana, and
Missouri. The Society chose the last state, possibly because
of the Germans already settled here.

They sent a schoolteacher, George Bayer, to buy a town
site surrounded by farmland. He came back with scattered
plots near the Missouri River, most of them wooded and
hilly. Among the properties Bayer purchased, however,
was an excellent steamboat landing. That encouraged back-
ers to hope their city would one day rival Philadelphia.

On this land the Philadelphia Society imposed its town

plan. Hermann was to have four public squares, two 150-foot wide promenades, and streets with names like Schiller, Gutenberg, Mozart, Goethe and Wien.

But when settlers arrived in late 1837, they disliked both the soil and the climate. Furthermore Bayer, who was supposed to superintend all the Society's eleven thousand acres — to survey, to assign property, to regulate complaints, to arrange for food and houses — was not up to his duties. The discord between agent and settlers soon became virulent.

After two rocky years the grandly conceived street grid only sketchily connected the town's eighty houses. Hermann's population of 450, though respectable in frontier terms, did not meet the goals set in Philadelphia. Disillusioned, the settlers severed relations with their eastern parent. It looked as if the hoped-for "Athens of the Midwest" would decline without even approaching its Golden Age.

Despite this initial disappointment, Hermann grew. By the 1850s the town, now a county seat linked to St. Louis by rail, had 1,400 inhabitants; the surrounding rural areas were developing around very German crossroad villages.

Take U.S. 40/Interstate 64 to Missouri 94. Head west almost fifty-six miles through varied but peaceful scenery toward the intersection of Missouri 94 and 19. After Treloar watch for river views and for a pristine white clapboard enclave on the left. This is the 1870 St. John's United Church of Christ and its parsonage, flanked by a graveyard.

Cross Missouri 19 and continue on Missouri 94 four miles to Rhineland, a shiny collection of massive metal silos on the right and clusters of small nineteenth-century houses on the left. Bluff buffs will want to continue six miles west to tiny Bluffton to admire the cedar-dotted 400-foot high escarpments which sit directly on the road, and then backtrack to the western edge of Rhineland.

Just outside Rhineland, P takes you a short distance
north to Starkenburg's St. Martin's Church, which appears
on the left. A good example of the Gothic Revival Germans
favored, the church was built in the 1870s. The interior has
an almost Mexican exuberance with its brightly painted
wooden stations of the cross, its turquoise-tinted capitals,
and the pastel colors of its windows.

To the south of the church lies the real attraction, the
Shrine of Our Lady of Sorrows. In the 1880s teenage
August Mitsch came here from Germany to assist his uncle,
Father Hoehn. In 1887 the youth found an abandoned
Madonna, the "white lady," in the attic. He was moved
first to place her under a dogwood tree and pay her
homage, then to build her a chapel.

In 1891, when heavy rains delayed harvests, the faithful
promised to honor the "white lady" if they stopped. The
sun came out; the Shrine of Our Lady of Sorrows was born.
In 1892 Hermannites began pilgrimages. Before long thousands participated in fall and spring ceremonies.

Within the 1910 stone structure German votive plaques
demonstrate the shrine's success. Lourdes water is available
in plastic phials. Notice the *intarsio faux-marbre* linoleum.

The whole complex — the church and chapels, the
grottos and the popsicle-shaped stations of the cross, the
outdoor altar and pews — would seem like a theme park,
were it not for the air of abandonment that hangs over all.
Starkenburg is for devotees of desuetude.

Return to Missouri 19 and turn right. As you cross the
Loutre and Missouri Rivers, Hermann on its bluff appears
before you.

After the bridge, head straight a few yards to Deutschheim, a state historic site still under restoration. Opposite,
in an island in Market Street, is the City Hall. On the other
side of City Hall are the Hermann Printing Company and
the German Haus Motel, both mid-nineteenth-century build-

ings. Market Street is a reminder of Hermann's founders' ambitions. Though modeled after the thoroughfare of the same name in Philadelphia, Hermann's is ten feet wider.[1]

Head right (west) on Second Street past the Strehly House, home of the first German newspaper west of St. Louis. At the end of Second the *Ausblick* affords fine river views.

Turn left, drive two blocks, and turn left again onto Fourth Street. The whitewashed stone house on the right dates from 1840. Opposite is the Old Rock Church, modest former home of Hermann Presbyterianism. Farther down Fourth is the grand St. George Catholic Church. The armor-clad figure in front of the rectory is, of course, St. George. But the statue's Roman garb brings to mind Hermann himself, a German tribal prince and one-time Roman soldier who crushed Roman legions in 11 A.D., thus becoming Germany's first national hero.

At Market turn right. Turn right again at Fifth Street. At the end of the first block is the Old School House. Note the white Gothic gem catercorner. At the end of the street, turn left onto Washington and right on Seventh. The 1843 Klinge Hotel and Horse Stable on the corner served farmers coming to market. Go one block to Goethe and turn left. The German Baroque Herzog place on the corner was built by a Stone Hill Winery president. It is now a guest house.

Continue on Goethe. At the end you will see the winery, established in 1847. Jog right, then follow the driveway up to the main building, which dates from 1869. Stone Hill was one of the largest wineries in the world before Prohibition. Its cellars, devoted to mushroom cultivation for forty years, were returned to their original use in the 1960s.

Tours of the cellars are available. Take the back way out, past the restaurant.

Turn left on Washington Street. Turn right on West 11th

Street then quickly left to admire the City Park's octagonal Rotunda, recently restored as a theater. Note also the pool, fair grounds, and playing fields in the park. For a town of fewer than 3,000 people, Hermann is well-equipped with public spaces and recreational facilities — a latter-day reflection of the Philadelphia Society's high civic aspirations.

Back on Washington, turn right. At 1006 stands another winery executive's elaborate 1885 dwelling.

Continue on Washington to Sixth Street. Turn right, noting the pleasant streetscape of old brick houses. At Market Street turn right, then left on Ninth Street. At the northeastern corner of the City Cemetery, turn right on Gutenberg. You'll see a sign marking the grave of George Bayer, the settlement society's agent. At his death in 1839, the still angry townspeople placed him as far as possible both from other graves and from the city he founded. Now, with the recognition of Hermann's success, reconciliation has taken place. His grave has become one of Hermann's sights.

Turn left on Twelfth Street. At the bottom of the hill turn left, then right across the bridge and right again onto unmarked Tenth Street just before a second bridge. Turn left on Gellert Street. On the way up, look to your left for glimpses of Hermann below. Just over the crest the river is visible. At Third and Gellert is the 1846 Klenk House. Turn left on Third, then right on Franklin, where there are several old homes.

Turn right down Second Street, left at the bottom of the hill and left again on First Street. Look for the Hermannhof Winery on the left, near Frene Creek. Like nearly all the central portion of Hermann, it is listed on the National Register of Historic Places. Tours are available here. You may enjoy Hermannhof's good picnic provisions in the enticing vine-shaded wine garden out back.

Continue down First and turn right on Gutenberg. The Festhalle too has been recently renovated in fine style by the

Hermannhof's owners, the Dierbergs. There is a golden stag out front and a pleasant entrance at back. Turn left on Wharf. Note the fine nineteenth-century White House Hotel.

Turn left on Schiller past the iron-balconied St. Charles Hall. Crossing First you will see Hermann's Concert Hall with its lyre and horn mural.

Continue on Schiller. To the right on Third is an intact nineteenth-century block. At the corner of Fourth and Schiller are, on the left, the Bay-Hermann Bank and, on the right, the Historic Hermann Museum, formerly the German School. The museum's curator is Kermitt Baeker, riverman on the boat *Missouri River*. The museum's River Room is a trove of lore and memorabilia.

The building itself is a reminder of the founders' desire to conserve German culture in Hermann. In the nineteenth century the town's Anglo-Americans learned the tongue of their neighbors in the natural course of things, as did the few blacks, masters of a beautiful Hermann German. Classes were taught in German well into the twentieth century.

Though anti-German feeling generated by the First World War ended that, the town nonetheless conserved its Germanness. The war's psychological adversity may even have helped unite townspeople. Prohibition, which followed in the twenties, isolated the winemaking community further. The Depression also had an immobilizing effect on a town already tight-knit in its old ways.

Hermann conserved a charm that had as much to do with its being a backwater as an Old World place.

One of the museum's exhibits is an original schoolroom. The persistence of Germanic discipline is suggested by an anecdote related by Burton Roueché, in his loving account of a visit here. This one is about the origins of Maifest. At the end of the school year the schoolchildren would be marched from the Old German School to the park, where the town band would play, sack races would be run, and a maypole would be decorated. Then "the treat" would unfold:

Everything was very disciplined. Hermann was totally German in those days, and all of us children spoke German before we learned English. . . . We would all line up and the bugler would blow a special call and we would march — very correctly — over to the table, and they would give each of us a big slice of knockwurst on a bun. Delicious! Then we'd march away, and in a few minutes the bugle would blow again, and off we'd go to the table once more. This time they would give us a glass of pink lemonade. And the pink was *wine*! Oh, my! Then one more bugle call and we'd each get an orange. We really looked forward to the Maifest. But they dropped it twenty years or more ago. It got so the children didn't think it was much of a treat anymore.[2]

Turn right for Fourth Street's tin facades and arcades and then right on Market and right again on First.

The Gasconade county courthouse on the left was a gift of a rich Hermannite at the end of the nineteenth century. The town, solidly Union as were all German communities in the Civil War, made its contribution to the cause with a green cannon named Ever True, now firmly mounted on the courthouse grounds. When Sterling Price's Confederate troops were advancing toward Hermann in October 1864, the few old men left here moved the cannon from one hill to another, their shots awakening fear in the rebels that they faced a numerous force.

Continue down First, whose small town feeling has not been disrupted; even the recent brick Hermann Eye Center and Fritz Auto Parts have maintained an appropriate scale.

Continue east on Missouri 100. Less than a mile out of town, on the left, is the beautiful complex of Beard's Wine Cellar Antiques, housed in the wine cellar of the 1860 estate of a prosperous Hermann brickmaker.

Go east over five miles on Missouri 100, watching for

the many nineteenth-century houses and barns, to B. Turn left for Berger, dominated by three octagonal church spires. The prettiest, the 1887 St. Pauluskirche, sits off B to the right. Berger is as German as Hermann.

Beyond town B curves to the right. The farmland here was reclaimed from the bed of the Missouri by silt-collecting wing dams, forming a Midwestern polder.

Turn right at the Bias Winery sign for a visit to this recently established but pleasant vineyard. Back on B, head east (right) for Etlah, a village which has all but disappeared. B reconnects with Missouri 100. Turn left (east).

Before long Missouri 100 enters New Haven, settled in 1805. Turn left on Douglas Street, which is just before the Boondocker Inn. Turn right on Melrose and left on Maupin, which winds past the VFW Hall to the Langenberg Hat factory. Turn right here on Wall Street, whose rich houses command a view of the Missouri. At the end of Wall turn left on Miller.

Turn right on Front Street, following the Boat Ramp sign, to the river access for a close-up of the Missouri. Backtrack on Front to Cottenwood and turn right. Turn left on Main Street. On the right are two freshly painted Victorian cottages. Turn left on Olive past the modest police station and city hall. Turn left on Front Street, an intact old main street with railroad views. Notice the snazzy Walt Theater and the barber shop. Turn right up Miller. At the top of the hill, after the Romanesque Church of the Assumption, veer left. Miller will take you to Missouri 100. Turn left.

Pick up Interstate 44 east at Union and return to St. Louis.

For information call:
Bias Winery 1-834-5475
Deutschheim State Historic Site 1-486-5532
Hermannhof Winery 1-486-5959
Historic Hermann Museum 1-486-2017
Stone Hill Winery 1-486-2221

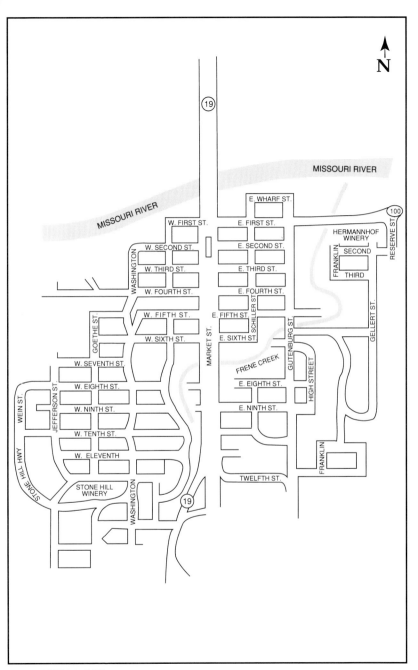

HERMANN

Fredericksburg Ferry

Begins at U.S. 50 and Missouri 19

Much of Hermann's Germanness lies in its urban quality
— its orderly grid, its close-to-the-sidewalk houses, and
its big town amenities. Even if Hermann did not become
the rival to Philadelphia its founders hoped, it did become
a city. But Missouri had another kind of pioneer German,
the farmer. A steady stream of rural Germans arrived here
in the 1800s; they transformed Missouri's wilderness into
a characteristically German landscape.

"No other race of people," William S. Bryan writes in
his 1876 *History of Pioneer Families of Missouri*, "ever did
more for the development of a country . . . they caused
barren hillsides to blossom with grape vines and fruit
trees, and opened large farms in the midst of dense forests.
Swamps and marshes were drained, and fertile fields took
the place of stagnant ponds that for years had sent out
their miasmas to poison the atmosphere of the surrounding country and breed fevers, chills, and pestilence. . . ."[1]

This tour takes you into a countryside where meadows
are graced by barns of Old World solidity and stone
houses nestle near oak-covered hillsides, evoking the
harmonies of early Renaissance painting.

Take Interstate 44 to the Union exit. U.S. 50 west takes
you through a string of towns along the Old State Road to
Jefferson City. After Rosebud, watch for stone and log
farmsteads on either side of the highway.

The tour proper begins at Drake, about sixty-seven

Bay Mercantile Company

miles from Interstate 270. After the Dutch Mill store on the left, keep right (it's really straight) for Missouri 19. Missouri 19 used to be the Old Iron Road, on which iron blooms from the Meramec Springs Iron Works were carted from St. James to Hermann from 1840 to 1860. Drake's position at its intersection with the Old State Road gave the now reduced village considerable prosperity.

On the left you will see the newly restored red brick general store and, opposite, the old frame steam-powered mill, now an antique shop. Beyond, on the right, is the red brick miller's house; farther still, on the left, is Zoar Methodist Church, with an interesting bell tower.

Turn around; opposite Zoar's driveway sits a nine-teenth-century frame house. The brick house next door has a log building behind. Backtrack to U.S. 50 and head west.

In four and a half miles a view of a fertile valley opens just before a pretty brick schoolhouse on the right. A majestic stone dwelling appears on the left about a mile and a half after.

A right on K to Bay leads you past wooden barns whose half hidden inner log walls are symptomatic of this area's relation with its history: the past is built on, not destroyed.

Grazing in the foreground, as you first glimpse Bay, are Charolais cattle, white against the meadows. Directly before you is the top of the steeple of one of Bay's three churches; framing it are nineteenth-century stone and wood buildings of medieval nobility. The building on the left was originally an 1870s' livery stable. The Bay Mercantile Company is on the right. The 1911 State Bank of Bay, just beyond to the left, has a pressed tin facade and a blue glass lightning rod/weather vane. Bay's mill, now dilapidated, is across W.

Turn right on W. A mile and a half beyond turn right on gravelled Little Bay Road and right again on Presbyterian Church Road. At the top of the hill the 1851 white stone Bethel Presbyterian Church, with a pressed tin steeple, stands in a grove of oaks. Its white frame outhouses, the red brick parsonage, and the cemetery beyond, complete a picture of peace.

Return to Little Bay Road and turn right. At the top of the hill another right takes you to the neatly restored parsonage and the 1867 St. Paul's Church, also stone but in a grove of cedars. It is in the hands of the Gasconade County Historical Society. Both parsonage and church command views of Bay.

Backtrack just beyond the parsonage to St. Paul's cemetery road. The road winds for a gentle half-mile over three creek crossings, perfectly respectful of its sublime setting. The geometry of the simple chapel and the rows of tombstones deepen the harmony. The stones seem to be arranged in series: here doves, there roses or clasped hands. Nearby benches make it a spot for a meditative picnic.

Back on St. Paul's Church Road turn right. Go to the bottom of the hill and turn right on Krull Road, which is unpaved and can be avoided by backtracking to W.

If you choose W, turn right to wind by neat farms. One of them, on the right, has a big 1848 stone barn whose narrow ventilation slits were left open in summer and stuffed with straw in winter. Once Herr Linneman, the builder of the barn, had picked out this land, he walked to the St. Louis land office for the deed, and then walked back: a three-day round-trip. At the intersection with F, turn left.

The even more beautiful Krull Road runs through a silent valley whose substantial stone and frame farms have a timeless quality. There is a magnificent barn on the right just after you turn, followed by the spruced-up Middlebrook farm on the left. After several bends in the road you come upon the Johnson farm. Not far is a beautifully sited cluster of butter-colored limestone structures, including a little tower with round windows — the smokehouse.

After this the scenery roughens with quarry scars and mobile homes. Krull Road ends at F, where you will turn left. Keep on F several miles to J, where you turn left again.

F reappears; you may want to turn right on it for Stolpe, positioned on the agreeable Gasconade River. As you enter the hamlet, note the old resort cabins — reminiscent of the one Clark Gable and Claudette Colbert visited in *It Happened One Night.* The road ends with a commercial camping site. Turn back and continue right on J.

One mile beyond is St. John's United Church of Christ, its octagonal steeple making a fine effect against the sky.

Born in 1884 as the Deutsche Evangelische St. Johannes Kirche, it has a German inscription within reminding us that "Selig Sind Die Gottes Wort Horen und Bewahren." Luke 11:28. — Blessed are they that hear the word of God and keep it. Not surprisingly the German Broadcasting Company found material here for a program on Missouri's German heritage.

A few miles farther on J is the Fredericksburg Ferry. Two dollars buys passage on the single car "Roy J," piloted by a charming Charon. The trip, all of a minute, is over when the boat bumps into the opposite shore. Fredericksburg, which was a shipping point for grain, cattle and hogs, is soon to have a restaurant in the old mill. The ferry landing also serves as Fredericksburg's swimming hole. The Gasconade's blue-green water, the willows, the "Roy J" and the old buildings make this, in its low-key way, as picturesque as anyplace in the world.

Follow the signs through the hamlet for J and turn right. At its intersection with OO is a deconsecrated church of extreme purity; the steeple is faced in corrugated tin now, but that doesn't detract from the building's perfect scale.

Follow OO to the crossroads village of Pershing, which was Potsdam until antipathy to all things German in World War I provoked a name change. The left fork, Buel Store Road, leads by frame houses and an old store and pump, offering "fortified gas"; look out at the river, then turn back. Take OO left by the 1912 St. Peter's Church. In a couple of miles appears the Rainbow Park lodge; here you can eat seven days a week, year round. Its interior sports neon beer signs, a ceiling that sparkles, and conversation about huntin', fishin', farmin', and fried foods. The rest rooms are for Bucks and Does.

Backtrack to J and turn left. At N turn right and then left at Missouri 100. After Bockting's tractor dealership,

watch for the apricot-colored Tara on the right. Take this
residential street past a cemetery. The street descends a
steep hill with gingerbread frame houses clinging to it.
This is Morrison.

At the bottom continue straight along Main Street. The
1900 Morrison Bank has become Pat's Small Engines. A
left at the MFA grain silo, left again a block later, and then
right, puts you back on Missouri 100. Turn left.

Several miles east is Gasconade City, even less prepos-
sessing than Morrison, despite its history. It was the
county seat and almost became state capitol. Turn left on
Fifth Street, the first you see. At the church turn right on
Oak Street, which takes you by the asphalt-papered City
Hall/Fire Department building.

How did the erstwhile capital of so fine a county fall so
low? Floods first washed the county seat away — to
another city. In 1855 the inaugural train from St. Louis to
Jefferson City, loaded with many of the state's elite,
crashed into the river when the bridge gave way, killing
thirty-three. The U.S. government boat yards were phased
out in the 1970s. Gasconade City has known more than its
share of misfortune; the number of bars at Oak's intersection with Second suggests the inhabitants know it.

Turn left on Second and cross the railroad tracks. At
the end of Second, which becomes gravel, stands an abandoned metal foundry; beyond it are the boat yards.
Behind these industrial ruins, the Gasconade's blue-green
waters flow into the muddy Missouri. A sign at the
confluence marks an 1804 Lewis and Clark campsite; it's
worth a stroll.

Backtrack on Second to Missouri 100, and turn left
toward the river. Cross it and ascend the wooded bluffs.
Once over them, look for a grand grey, white, and red
farm on the left.

The white complex a distance beyond on the left

signals your approach to Hermann: it was the poor house, an institution provided for in the town's early planning. Farther on we again see substantial stone farmsteads. On the left watch for an 1858 German house with creole porch. Half a mile beyond on the right is a tightly built 1855 house. Yet another limestone construction is snuggled into the hillside on the left, a little farther on.

Follow Missouri 100 to the edge of Hermann. Turn right on Missouri 19, then at once left on H to continue this bucolic drive. The scenery here, marked with fine brick and stone structures, is vaster than any we have seen today. Follow H to E and turn left for Stony Hill's white church, with a multicolored steeple. Its compact brick predecessor stands just beyond.

You can continue on E to Missouri 100, thence back to St. Louis. If your appetite for farmhouses, churches and rural views is not satiated, and you have some extra time, follow E to Y, where a right takes you (a little deviously) to YY. YY tangles with C at an uneasy intersection but follow it east to A, where a right (south) takes you to Union. Pick up U.S. 50 east to I-44 home.

For information call:
Fredricksburg Ferry 1-294-7203

Methodist church, Labadie

Begins at U.S. 40/Interstate 64 and Olive Boulevard

What gives some towns that elusive quality, a sense of place? In the natural course of things, a settlement's identity has to do with its ethnic background, its relation to the land, and its social and economic functions. The origins of a place's identity are normally the subject of history and archaeology. But in modern America we can sometimes witness the creation of identity even as it happens.

You usually approach Chesterfield, which was incorporated as a city in 1988, on U.S. 40/I-64. This road, especially toward St. Louis, has the region's best collection of highway architecture. Buildings conceived with cars in mind tend to have certain characteristics. Their perspective is skewed lengthwise to give passing motorists a chance to see them. They often have sleek, aerodynamic exteriors and quantities of reflective glass. These surfaces, mirroring the light of the sky, obliterate space — and therefore a sense of place — much as the automobile does. Highway architecture's "place" is motion, its identity is whatever can be intuited through the window of a speeding car.

Today's Chesterfield is inconceivable without the superhighway, thanks to which it has grown to a city of more than thirty thousand inhabitants. Yet for a community that wants to become *someplace*, as Chesterfield definitely does, highway architecture presents a problem. New technology means that these streamlined constructs can be put up anywhere. But identity, by definition, is specific. If you're trying to strengthen it, you cannot use the generic elements that go anyplace, because they create no place.

The gap between speed and community is not as abstract as it sounds. People may work well enough in a traffic corridor, but the only one they ever wanted to live on was the Grand Canal. Where there is no sense of place, disorientation is inevitable. The absence of stable landmarks has a counterpart in human lives called anomie, the moral drift that is as much a consequence of mobility as is highway architecture.

There is evidence that Chesterfield wants to avoid that. Barely a month after incorporation the new city's government set up both an architectural review board and an historical commission. Beauty and authenticity may have some political priority here.

The city's decision to locate its government center in the Stemme Office Park, at least for now, is significant. To see this, turn right off U.S. 40 onto Olive, noting the two convex brick and glass structures on either side of the road. Turn right again onto Roosevelt Parkway. The not yet completed Stemme complex, work of St. Louis architects Mackey and Associates, says much about Chesterfield's desire to establish an identity.

The name itself is not the euphonic invention of a real estate developer but that of the family who farmed this land long before anyone dreamed Chesterfield would become what it is today. This agreeable gesture toward authenticity is repeated in the architecture, which respects St. Louis' solid brick and stone tradition, as well as human scale. The complex not only resolutely faces away from the superhighway, it is to become a spacious enclosure with two more buildings forming a gateway on Conway Road.

Perhaps the most telling element is the pergola or portico connecting the buildings; almost meaningless from the road, it is pleasant to walk under. This is the opposite of highway architecture.

Chesterfield has a Comprehensive Plan which is to "insure that Chesterfield fulfills its promise of becoming a total community." The Stemme portico, appreciable only by people on foot, brings to mind the Plan's provision for sidewalks along the city's boulevards. It is enough to recall that Ladue prohibits sidewalks as inharmonious with its rural character. Chesterfield is that new phenomenon, the urban village.[1] Sidewalks presuppose people on foot, and someplace to go.

Just to the north of Stemme is a fine example of the sort of building and atmosphere this area produced in the past. Backtrack to Olive and turn right a short distance for Faust Park, on the left. The well-intentioned shelter for an old carousel is an unhappy exercise, architecturally speaking. Newly sited nearby are a number of old structures moved here from elsewhere. Such "historic" villages of singly authentic structures don't collectively represent the truth of the past. Yet they are interesting, and since the buildings were moved here not for commercial exploitation but to preserve them from destruction, the effort is commendable.

One structure here has the power of place Chesterfield aspires to. The beautifully sited Thornhill, on the park's south edge, was built around 1817 by Frederick Bates, who later became Missouri's second governor. Reminiscent of houses in Bates' native Virginia, the well-wrought dwelling has been restored by the St. Louis County Department of Parks and Recreation. There are log outbuildings, and a cemetery where Bates is buried.

Backtrack on Olive toward U.S. 40 and continue south on Clarkson Road past the Chesterfield Mall. Turn right about a half mile after the mall and its adjacent shopping centers on Baxter Road, which you may cruise up and back on. Here Chesterfield returns to the urban village mode. The population density of these apartment blocks must be worthy of a city.

Return to Clarkson and turn left. Left again on Chesterfield Village Parkway, which will take you by the new brick YMCA, another Mackey creation, first of a series of civic buildings planned here.

Continue on the parkway to Chesterfield Airport Road, where you turn left. After passing through a rare old section of this new city, you come to the Smoke House, a good place for sausages and meats, and the first of many gourmet possibilities on this tour. If you want a picnic, this is the place for provisions.

Missouri's dislike of pretensions survives despite the snazzy image Chesterfield tries to project. When asked at a Chesterfield Historical Society meeting how the city got its name — so like the tony ones real estate developers invent — one woman answered that it referred either to a hog or a potato, she wasn't sure which. In fact, Chesterfield was long in use for a rural locality whose post office absorbed others around it.

Better names occur on the western edge of the twenty-seven square mile city. Here you have the Spirit of St. Louis Airport, familiarly known as "Spirit." Used for private planes, it justifies that otherwise astonishing declaration sometimes heard on local executive's lips, "We're flying out of Spirit."

Turn left on Long Road which takes you past a post-modern fire department. Just beyond is a cemetery with the best name, Gumbo, so called no doubt for the quality of the soil.

Turn right onto Wild Horse Creek Road (CC). This too is a real name, from some unruly nineteenth-century steed. There are horse farms here even now, but suburban creep threatens.

After three miles, turn left on C, then right, less than a mile farther, on Missouri 109. A mile and a half beyond is the Dr. Edmund A. Babler Memorial State Park, which dates from 1934. Its handsome structures were built by the Civilian Conservation Corps. Babler was a medical benefactor; his statue half a mile from the entrance features sickly stone figures striving to touch the hem of his bronze robe.

Babler's rugged terrain marks the border between the Ozarks and the glacial plain north of the Missouri River. After the last Ice Age, dust from newly exposed alluvial mud flats was blown onto the ridges here, making a deep, rich loess soil that accounts for the park's unusually impressive forests. The park is well endowed for sports, camping, picnics, and hiking.

Backtrack the short distance to the intersection of CC and C (that is, at Babler's entrance turn left onto Missouri 109 and then left onto C). Turn left on Wild Horse Creek Road (CC).

Soon views open up left and right, followed by farms. After another mile or so the road descends toward the creek bed where it winds along the boundary of Babler State Park. About two miles beyond note the abandoned 1859 stone church on your right.

Soon after, bear right on Ossenfort Road. Two more miles brings you to T; turn right. Veer right less than a mile and a half beyond at the signs for St. Albans and Malmaison.

The large stone barn with its round corner towers that appears in another mile and a half on the right was, like the buildings of St. Albans itself, part of a 5,200-acre estate owned by the shoe manufacturing Johnsons. St. Albans' cream and green frame buildings remain now as they were when part of the Johnson fief, but a country club and residential development are planned. The developers

developers promise that "Those homes will really reflect country living on a world-class golf course. There will be nothing like this in St. Louis." The houses on the golf course will have to be exceptional to make those who have loved St. Albans' idyllic nature not regret the change.

Founded by Peter Kincaid in 1837, St. Albans was settled by Germans. It attracted St. Louis' German-American architect Theodore Link, who in turn interested the Johnsons in the spot.

The 1893 Head's General Store has good sandwiches, but these are no competition for Malmaison, just across the bridge. Excellent French cuisine is served in this restaurant, built around an 1840 barn. Turn left after the bridge, noting stone cooling rooms built into the hillside,

General store, Labadie

then turn left again to cross another bridge. Turn right at the intersection and notice the red roof of the Johnson manse up on the hill to your right.

Turn right up the hill on T at the next intersection. A short distance beyond, the view opens up to include a huge Union Electric plant in the distance. At the bottom of the hill stands an old brick industrial structure.

T brings you to Labadie. Turn right at the stop sign to admire Labadie's downtown, which looks like a well-scrubbed white frame stage set. Along with restored shops there is Hunter's Hollow, a good restaurant.

Take the first left, Washington Street. Note the Methodist Church, with its splendid belfry, and the white frame cottage on the corner of Washington and Third. Turn left on Third and right on T.

Not quite two miles beyond note the 1868 Bethel Methodist Church and, farther on, the red roofed farmhouse, both on the right.

Red roofs were habitual in Hanover. Their presence here is a sign of German immigration. In fact in 1833 twelve Catholic Hanoverian families arrived in St. Louis with intentions of settling in Illinois. But they tired of waiting for a steamboat bound for the Illinois River. At the suggestion of a companion who had read Duden, they boarded one for the Missouri River, asking to be let off on the northern shore near Marthasville. When they were approaching this area, it was already growing dark. The captain suggested it was better to stop in Washington, where they were sure to find lodgings. The hotel owner, Herr Fricke, was German, one of Washington's first permanent residents. The Hanoverians must have struck up a friendship with him, for they stayed on in Washington, camping in a smokehouse near their compatriot the first winter.

Almost two miles beyond, turn right onto Missouri 100,

which continues through pleasant countryside. After five miles turn right onto East Fifth Street (South Point Road). The second house on the right, one-story brick with peaked roof and Federal detailing, is a fine example of a nineteenth-century German dwelling. Once a farm house, it is now on the edge of Washington. Another such house, one of many you will see here, sits farther down, also on the right. Follow East Fifth into Washington.

Sited at the southernmost point of the Missouri River, Washington at first was no more than a ferry landing. Yet the surrounding area was populated and prosperous. William Owens saw the place's possibilities, and at the end of the 1820s began selling lots. Unfortunately, in 1834 he was shot in the back, presumably by a forger he was to testify against. His death created legal entanglements delaying further settlement. His widow and son-in-law eventually resolved the difficulties; Lucinda Owens officially founded Washington in 1839. The town quickly got down to business and grew rich with shipping, milling, brick making, farm implements, merchandising, cigars, meat packing, as well as with the manufacture of hats, pipes, and zithers.

Just before a Hardee's, 2.7 miles after turning off Missouri 100, a right on Locust takes you past a collection of brick residences. At East Main look to your right, where, at the end of the street is Lucinda Owen's 1838 house. Go left on East Main, noticing the brick cottage at 204. Around the corner, at 2 Walnut, is the home of zither maker Franz Schwarzer.

Schwarzer was born in Austria and trained as a woodworker. He emigrated to America in 1864 and began manufacturing zithers full time in 1869. In 1873 he sent a sampling of his best work — which incorporated spruce, Missouri walnut, and hard maple — to the World's Fair in Vienna where he received a gold medal.

The zither company continued after Schwarzer's death in 1904. In 1919 a national gathering of zitherists was held and Schwarzer's home was named the "Zitherists' Shrine."

Continue on Main to Market, where you turn right, then left on Front Street. Here is the Missouri River, where the ferry landing that gave the town its name existed from 1820. The 1848 rush to California gold brought an increase in river traffic and a good deal of business to Washington. More gold hunters passed through on the way to Montana in the 1860s.

Note the 1889 Victorian water works, now a sculpture gallery. At the corner of Front and Lafayette is the 1846 Foss House, Washington's oldest frame building. This is the first of a series of bed and breakfasts on Front Street. The Washington House, once the best hotel between St. Louis and Kansas City, started out as Fricke's.

Note the gentrified old train station at Front and Cedar. The Langenberg Hat Company at 320 Front Street sports a trompe l'oeil mural.

Zither making was not Washington's most exotic industry. At Front and Cedar is the Missouri Meerschaum Company, where the world's supply of corn cob pipes is manufactured.

Dutch woodworker Henry Tibbe arrived here in the 1860s. He made spinning wheels and furniture until, at the request of a local farmer, he turned the first corn cob pipe. After that he set about improving the design, as have his successors. Now a special breed of thick-cobbed corn is used. The factory, established in 1872, is still in use.

Anton Tibbe, the founder's son, was instrumental in bringing electricity to the county. The Tibbe Electric Power House just beyond the Meerschaum building was designed by Theodore Link.

Continue on Front past more bed and breakfasts to the

imposing 1839 Elijah McLean house — yet another restaurant and inn.

A block beyond turn left up the hill on High Street and left again onto Second. Note here how the single-story German brick house has mutated into a 1930s bungalow. Note too the brick industrial structure farther down, once International Shoe, now Pendaflex. Late-twentieth century Washington's commercial and industrial base has remained as strong and varied as it was in the nineteenth century, thanks to vigorous local efforts to keep it that way.

On the southeast corner of Second and Stafford sits the 1860s home of Frank Stumpe, brick maker. There is a tall, narrow smokehouse in back.

Turn right on Stafford and left on Third, which boasts several nineteenth-century brick houses.

Turn left on Cedar and note the 1934 St. Francis Borgia Auditorium with its beige camouflage tile. Turn right onto Main Street. On the corner is the handsome 1884 St. Francis Borgia School and the 1869 church. Its stained glass windows and newly restored interior are worth climbing the stairs for. From the entrance you can see across the Missouri to Dutzow's St. Vincent's Church.

If a city, like a person, has an identity, then the downtown is the city's face. Washington is close enough to metropolitan St. Louis to have suffered some exurban sprawl. But city fathers — and mothers, since women generally have done more in historical preservation than men — have kept the center of town active. Washington's downtown is as alive as Hermann's downtown. Promotional literature assures us that "there's something for everyone" here — and the variety of enterprises bears that claim out. The literature notes Washingtonians' aim "to preserve the town's proud past for its promising future," a goal also being accomplished.

Turn right on Elm. Don't let its bustle distract you from 113's pressed tin Mannerist facade with gilt trim or from Cowan's restaurant, whose sturdy meals and ineffable pies deserve a pause.

Turn left on Third, left on Oak and right on Main, which, like Elm, is dense with businesses. A right onto Jefferson takes you past several fine brick buildings. Note especially the brick pilasters and blue and white trim at 212 Jefferson.

Follow Jefferson out of town, passing the elaborate Second Empire VFW building at Jefferson and Busch.

Go left (east) on Missouri 100. Just before the junction with Interstate 44, about ten miles out of Washington, curve left with Missouri 100 for the Shaw Arboretum at Gray Summit.

The Arboretum is both a reaction and an antidote to urban problems. In the 1920s soft coal fumes began to destroy the Missouri Botanical Garden in St. Louis, which bought land here to save their collections. By the end of the 1930s city pollution had been reduced enough for the garden to remain at its original site. The Arboretum's unusually varied landscape offered opportunities impossible in an urban setting. Purchases in the 1970s enlarged the facility to a total of nearly four square miles on either side of the Meramec. The garden's trails lead to an experimental prairie, to bluffs which command extensive views, to the Pinetum — the most extensive collection of conifers in the Midwest, and through woodlands rich with wildflowers.

Take I-44 home.

For information call:
Dr. Edmund A. Babler Memorial State Park 1-458-3813
Faust Park 532-7298
Gray Summit Arboretum 577-5138
Thornhill 889-3356

North Main Street, Hannibal

Begins at Interstate 70 and Missouri 79

You might expect that seeing Mark Twain memorabilia would be the best reason for a trip to Hannibal. As it turns out, of the strong attractions on this itinerary, the Twain material is the most swiftly dispatched. You are likely to want to linger more over the river towns' nineteenth-century architecture. Then there is the Mississippi itself, on this stretch truly majestic.

The names of the first streams Missouri 79 crosses — Peruque, Belleau, and Cuivre — demonstrate yet again how extensive the French presence was in Missouri. No one knows why they named the Peruque "wig." As mystifying is what you see on the left after about four miles on Missouri 79, an Aztec science-fiction fantasy whose candy-striped cylinders rotate at different velocities. It is the O'Fallon water treatment plant.

At eleven miles the sign for a nineteenth-century hamlet, Old Monroe, suggests the Anglo-Southern background of this area's settlers.

Nurseries begin to appear just after Foley. Fruit trees thrive on this region's well-drained loess-rich river bluffs. Missouri apples have long enjoyed renown; Mother Duchesne sent them as gifts to New Orleans.

At 25.5 miles appear the Champ Goodwood Farms, worth slowing down for. On the right you see a formal arrangement of silos and barn, and on the left a succession of barns with cupola-like vents of a surprisingly Gothic effect. Another beautiful farm sits in a fine grove less than two miles to the north, on the right side of Missouri 79.

At forty-three miles from the beginning of Missouri 79 you enter Clarksville. Settled in 1807, this village had the first macadam roads west of the Mississippi; perhaps that's how it became the site of the International Bicycle Races in 1887. Despite Clarksville's small population — little over 500, the same as in 1860 — civic enterprise is still alive here, as you will see. To the right as you enter the town is the Apple Shed, a busy cultural center.

Go right on Virginia Street opposite the library to First Street, which parallels the river. Turn left on First. Here and on Howard, three blocks down, the city is restoring nine buildings. The riverside park, with its picnic canopies and purple martin houses, is also attractive. Just after the cast iron commercial row, in restoration as we write, cross the train tracks for Lock and Dam 24.

Here views up and down the river vie with the hypnotic hydraulics of the lock and dam system, which enables Mississippi barges to descend from St. Anthony's Falls, Minnesota, to Alton, a drop of 420 feet.

Turn back. Go right on First a short block, then left up Mississippi to Second Street, Missouri 79. The neo-steamboat-Gothic Visitors Center at the corner houses a little collection of historical items, serving also as an observation post for the bald eagles that winter near the dam. Once headed for extinction, the birds represent an environmental success. Since the ban on DDT, their numbers have grown to the point where their survival seems assured. Across the street is a skylift which, for a fee, will take you to the highest spot along the Mississippi. Whether or not you go up, there are plenty of splendid views farther north.

For a quick turn through the increasingly spiffy Clarksville, turn left on Missouri 79 and right on Kentucky. At the end of the block sits a mid-nineteenth-century blacksmith shop. Turn right on Third. At what looks like the end of the street, jog right past an 1886 Victorian Gothic church. Curve with Third up the hill. A right on Howard — this is a picturesque corner — and a left on Missouri 79 take you out of town.

The peaceful views northward are broken by the Dundee Cement complex near Clarksville, then, near Louisiana, by the lemon smoke of the Hercules Missouri Chemical Works and by the riverside Bunge silos.

A small town, Louisiana is rich in historical architecture, both industrial and domestic. Just after Missouri 79 crosses the railroad tracks, turn right on Illinois and left on Main, where that mix is most apparent. A right on South Carolina and a left on Water take you past the American Shell Co., formerly the Nord-Buffum Pearl Button Co. Sometimes you can see a pile of shells in the parking lot. Currently American Shell exports these freshwater mussel shells to Japan, where they are used in creating cultured pearls. The company plans to revive the button industry, once thriving here.

Follow the riverside parking lot one block, enjoying the view, and return to Water Street. Drive a couple of blocks north on Water. Turn left on Tennessee and then right on Main, whose succession of handsome nineteenth-century houses ends with Riverview Park. Drive through the park for splendid views north and south. Turn left at the end of the park (Noyes Street) and left again onto Third, lined with more nineteenth-century houses; 220 Third is especially grand.

At the intersection of Third and Georgia you have a nearly intact commercial Victorian streetscape. Turn right. You may want to make a longish detour west on Georgia to the Stark Log Cabin, a little over two miles from here. If you do so note especially Governor Stark's house at 1401 and an antebellum mansion at 2009. The cabin itself

Mississippi River, Clarksville

is engaging; nearby are the headquarters of Stark Nurseries. Founded in 1816 by the Kentucky-born son of a friend of Daniel Boone, the nurseries are famous for having developed apples like the Delicious and, most recently, the Gala.

To continue the tour, go right (north) on Fourth, past both frame and rosy brick nineteenth-century dwellings, to Mansion. A left here and a right soon after put you back on Missouri 79.

Between Louisiana and Hannibal the Mississippi has a storybook quality. The highway department's marked scenic views are just that. Our favorite, the second marked one, is about twenty-two miles north of Louisiana.

Thirty-six miles from Louisiana, at an electrical substation on the left, is the entrance to the much advertised Mark Twain Cave where Tom Sawyer and Becky Thatcher were lost. The cave has geological as well as literary interest, for it is a dry maze; it has complex passages, but no large rooms or water systems. Even bigger is Cameron Cave, where lantern tours are offered in the summer.

A short distance north on Missouri 79, a brown sign directs you to Lover's Leap, so called for the usual Indian legend of thwarted love and suicide. A true story about the bluff is even less credible. In 1843 a religious group, convinced that the world was coming to an end, gathered here to await their ascension. That did not take place. They returned on October 22, 1844, when heaven again failed to open up, despite their long white robes.

From here Hannibal looks like the town Samuel Clemens described — "compact and nestled" between this cliff and Cardiff Hill, the "delectable place" to the north.

The pretty site does not suggest the town's initial relation to disaster. Abraham Bird got the land as recompense for his losses in the 1811 New Madrid earthquake; Hannibal then grew thanks to the flood-induced failure of its nearby rival, Marion City.

Come down off Lover's Leap and turn right into town. Cross town and turn right just before the stoplight and bridge ramp at Cardiff Hill. This is North Street. The hill's dilapidated and defunct lighthouse commemorates the 100th anniversary of Clemens' birth. At its foot a bronze group represents Huck and Tom. The Visitors Center, at North and Main, has a well-narrated slide show about Samuel Clemens, along with much memorabilia.

Across the asphalt, through the gate in a stone wall built in the late 1930s as a protection against fire — Cruikshank's Lumber Yard occupied the adjacent area — is Clemens' boyhood home, built by his lawyer father in 1844. Clemens senior was highly respected but unsuccessful financially. The family was not even able to hold on to this modest house.

You enter the backdoor. This is symptomatic of the indirect quality of much of Twain tourism in Hannibal. But there is a consolation in this approach: the first thing you see is the bedroom window through which Clemens escaped for night prowls with Huck Finn's inspiration, Tom Blankenship. Tom's signal was a meow.

Headphones along the way are informative. Still it's hard to overcome the feeling that you are in an aquarium. Tourism engineering has yet to evolve a way of preserving the domesticity of a house 140,000 people a year want to visit.

But Twain's spirit does come through in the displays that complete the tour; notice his plain white jacket, for instance, or his desk, almost as simple as Mother Duchesne's. Then there is the plaque with his remark, "Always do right. This will gratify some people and astonish the rest."

One wonders what Samuel Clemens would have thought of this inevitably fetishizing procedure. He might simply have observed that "Truth is the most valuable thing we have. Let us economize it."

The museum cannot be accused of economizing on the truth. But step into Hill Street. The white frame buildings around you are survivors of Clemens' town. Yet their theme park accoutrements destroy what they purport to commemorate. Part of the problem is signage. Across the street is the dwelling of Laura Hawkins, Sam's childhood sweetheart. Future writer Clemens loved Laura truly: he deliberately misspelled a word so that she would win a spelling bee. See how garishly this place of delicate connotations is advertised. Real life is reduced to a studio tour.

The best way to remember Twain is to reread his fiction.

In truth the writer's "white town drowsing" was lost long before Hannibal chose to cash in on him. The late-nineteenth-century lumber and manufacturing boom dwarfed Twain's village.

Disproportion now rules Hill Street more than ever: the bridge high on the left, the silos on the right, not to mention the Mark Twain Dinette's giant rotating root beer mug, impose dollhouse status on the Clemens-era buildings. An ill-conceived marina also falsifies the town's relation to the river.

At the corner of Main and Hill is Grant's Drug Store, a prefabricated Greek Revival structure restored to its 1840 appearance. Inside you can see nineteenth- and early-twentieth-century pharmaceutical tools and other artifacts. A dime will get you an explanation of some of the objects.

The stretch of buildings opposite the drug store gives an idea of what commercial Hannibal looked like in the late-nineteenth century. One of these houses, Ole Planter's, is a plain but good place to eat.

If the Twain memorials are inevitably a little disappointing, Hannibal does offer a genuine treat. Its Victorian urban fabric is surprisingly intact west of Main. There are no architectural or historical stars here, just an impressive array of Italianate and Queen Anne houses.[1]

Go south on Main to Broadway and turn right. Numbers 306-308 still display their original 1873 storefronts and cornice. A peek into 308 gives you a glimpse of a rich but abandoned 1908 interior. The St. Louis firm of Barnett, Haynes and Barnett designed the lushly decorated City Hall, at the corner of Fourth and Broadway.

Turn right on Fourth Street. At 213 is Trinity Episcopal Church which has several Tiffany windows. 321 North Fourth is also noteworthy. Turn left a block farther on North Street and left again on North Fifth. Note 415's fine little porch high above the street.

One of Hannibal's many rich lumbermen built the 1889 mansion at 313 North Fifth. Across the street at 312 is a beautifully restored 1870 brick house. Just after Center Street at 121 North Fifth is the former Park Theater, where Maude Adams and Lillian Russell once trod the boards.

At Broadway turn right, and right again at Sixth Street. Note the 1884-88 Old Federal Building at 600 Broadway. At 215 North Sixth Street, 521 Bird Street (just across Sixth) and 300 North Sixth Street (just across Bird) is a cluster of Italianate houses. At 401 North Sixth is a beautiful peach and white Queen Anne structure.

Turn left here on Hill Street and left again on North Seventh and continue to Broadway. Go left on Broadway and right on Fourth Street. At the corner of Church and Fourth observe the 1878 Old Police Station and Jail; there used to be two onion domes. Right one block, at Fifth and Church, is the 1901 Garth Memorial Free Library. It contains an excellent portrait of young Samuel Clemens.

At 512 Church is the reason for the street's name: the 1854 white brick Immaculate Conception Chapel. 120 South Sixth, at the corner, is the 1869 rectory. Go left on Sixth, through a plain but homogeneous block.

Continue south across the railroad tracks. You are now on the wrong side of them. Drive over Bear Creek and to the top of the hill. These small run-down houses in their bucolic setting (watch for grazing sheep) are reminiscent of pre-boom Hannibal. Tom Sawyer would have felt more at home here than on North Sixth Street.

Turn around. Just after the railroad tracks make a left on Colfax. A right on Seventh takes you past the once flourishing International Shoe Company, a grand though ghostly reminder of turn-of-the-century Hannibal's transition from lumber to manufacturing center. By the time the forests of Michigan and Minnesota were exhausted, Hannibal produced paint, stoves, street car fenders, furniture, barrels, cold storage equipment, painted china, cured hams, wine and beer.

Factories shared the industrial corridor along Bear Creek with the railroads' car shop and wheel foundry, fruits of the town's early railroad interest. The first locomotive built west of the Mississippi was completed here in 1865 and the world's first railroad mail car followed some years later.

Go left after the factory and right on unmarked Eighth, which looks more like a truck parking lot than a street.

Three blocks north at Center and Eighth is the 1872 Baptist Church, the black community's oldest landmark. By the 1860s approximately 40 percent of Hannibal's population was black, most of them working in the lumber industry.

At the end of Eighth, turn left on Bird. On your right appears the entrance to J. J. Cruikshank's Rockcliffe Mansion, most opulent product of Hannibal's lumber wealth. Wind up the steep drive for a 45-minute tour of this Gilded Age dwelling. If you're not a fan of late Victorian grandeur and gloom, you may find the McKnight House, next door on the left, prettier.

Exit at the rear of the house and turn left on Hill Street. Take the first left, Stillwell Place. Clemens was fêted at no. 9 in 1902 during his last Hannibal visit. At the first intersection, jog slightly to the left onto Maple. Turn left at Center where 1020, 1016 and 1000 deserve a look.

Make a right on Tenth Street. At Broadway look to your left for the 1900 Marion County Courthouse.

That completes the tour of Hannibal proper. There are two interesting possibilities for your return to St. Louis. The fastest is U.S. 61, which also permits a look at another beautiful mansion. Turn right on Broadway and left at the second stoplight. This street, Business 61, joins U.S. 61 in about three miles. Head south a half mile and turn left at the large red and white sign for Garth Mansion. Smaller signs lead you right about a mile on a gravel road to Woodside, the 1871 summer home of John Garth and his wife, friends of Samuel Clemens. It is now a bed and breakfast establishment. Return to U.S. 61 and drive south for St. Louis.

That's the quickest way. But a more beautiful route offers the chance of seeing other examples of fine nineteenth-century architecture. Take Missouri 79 back south to Clarksville and turn right on W, Kentucky Street. Almost immediately out of town a red brick Federal house appears on the right, the first of many. Especially grand dwellings stand at 1.5 and 3.9 miles from Clarksville. At five miles turn right on WW. Four and a half miles beyond, turn left on D. After just over three miles turn left on H and, a tenth of a mile later, left into the gravel drive of the 1856 St. John's Episcopal Church. The compact building is both strong and graceful; look through a window at the simple interior, its altar inscribed with the words "Holy, Holy, Holy." Backtrack to D which goes south through Eolia and joins U.S. 61 shortly thereafter. From the beginning of W to the intersection of U.S. 40/Interstate 64 and Interstate 270 is seventy-four miles.

For information call:
Cameron Cave 1-221-1656
Clarksville Visitors Center 242-9662
Grant's Drugstore 1-221-2477
Hannibal Visitors Center 1-221-2477
J.J. Cruikshank's Rockcliffe Mansion 1-221-4140
Mark Twain Boyhood Home 1-221-2477
Mark Twain Cave 1-221-1656
Skylift 242-3711
Stark Log Cabin 1-754-5511

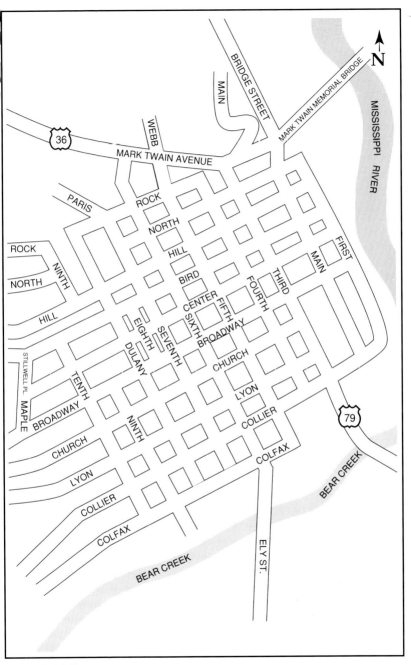

HANNIBAL

Haskell Playhouse, Alton

Begins at Interstate 270 and Illinois 3

History and nature do not always accord one another their deserved respect. That goriest of battles, Pilot Knob, took place in the most idyllic of valleys. The beautiful region of Illinois traversed by this tour likewise suggests a disparity between the works of men and the works of nature.

It begins, however, not with tragedy but with irony. About three miles north of I-270 on Illinois 3, turn left at the New Poag Road stoplight for the Lewis and Clark Historic Site. The road passes through a swampy stretch alongside Wood River. It is a sad-looking low place.

But it's not as low as where the Lewis and Clark's first camp actually was. That is now underwater, victim of a shift in the river. The spot belonged, incidentally, to Nicholas Jarrot, whose house still stands in Cahokia.

In a sense even the true Camp Dubois, so-called from the French name for the river, was on the wrong site. You would expect the great westward expedition to have begun on the west bank of the Mississippi. But history overcame logic even as, later, nature over-whelmed history. Lewis and Clark's men had to camp on the east bank the first winter because in St. Louis Lieutenant Governor de Lassus had not got official notice of the Louisiana Purchase. He refused to let the Americans across. Only in May 1804, after five months at Camp Dubois, was the Corps of Discovery able to proceed.

The monument is in keeping with the swamp and the pothole road: you might mistake it for a restroom. The eleven cement pylons commemorate the future states touched by the expedition.

So flat and featureless is the terrain that the Missouri's entrance here into the Mississippi is barely noticeable, an anticlimax for America's second-longest river. Only a difference in color marks the rivers' confluence. But there is a great movement of barges on the water.

Continue north on Illinois 3 midst a peculiar swamp, farm, and industrial landscape. On the right, white holding tanks with domes, pipes, and stacks mimic mosques and minarets. Just over three miles north of the Lewis and Clark site, also on the right, is a pale blue, yellow, and pink complex, encrusted with catwalks and stairs.

Note on the left the huge grassy earthwork protecting these low-lying lands from the river. Veer left onto Illinois 143, the Great River Road. The dike continues, a long minimalist sculpture interrupted by glimpses of the Mississippi through the floodgates. Drive three miles on Illinois 143 and turn left at the stoplight for Lock and Dam 26. A visitor center — observation deck, river museum, theater and gift shop — is scheduled to open here in 1993. Until then wooden shelters allow views of the enormous concrete complex which spans the river.

Lock and Dam 26 is only the latest of the U.S. Army Corps of Engineers' many interventions on the Mississippi. In the early-nineteenth century, West Point alone trained engineers. Congress naturally turned to the Army in 1824 to improve navigation along the river. The Corps accomplished that by removing snags. In 1878 Congress authorized a four-and-a-half-foot river channel to facilitate shipping. The Corps responded by removing rapids and other hazards, and digging lateral canals around especially dangerous sections. In 1907 a six-foot channel was authorized. The Corps installed a series of wing dams, forcing the river into a narrower and therefore deeper channel. In the 1930s Congress approved a plan of locks and dams from Minneapolis to St. Louis, making a nine-foot channel possible. Since then river traffic has increased steadily.

Lock and Dam 26, so near the mouths of the Missouri and Illinois rivers, is an especially busy point in this system. In 1974 the Corps published plans for two 1,200-foot locks to replace the 1938 facility. After a battle with environmentalists, the Corps got approval for one such lock. This lock passes the long multi-barge tows used nowadays in a half hour. The old facilities, splitting tows that had then to be reassembled, took three times as long.

That makes the new lock appear advantageous — and to the barge industry it is. But environmentalists argue that for everyone else the new lock and dam could be a disaster, a step toward expansion of the entire Mississipi system.

No one knows the full effects of lock and dam expansion, or of the deeper channel environmentalists fear will accompany it. But some things are clear. Damming rivers disrupts wetland habitats. After an initial benefit of increased water levels, sloughs tend to fill with silt; seasonal flooding can no longer scour them.

Dredging to maintain the present nine-foot channel contributes to the silt problem, both by churning up the waters and by the erosion of spoilage piles dumped carelessly along the banks.

River traffic aggravates the silting. Increasingly affected, for instance, is the paddlefish. A caviar producing species almost unchanged since the Paleozoic era, the paddlefish swims with its broad, flat snout open to catch plankton and crustaceans. Its sole relative is in the Yangtze River — like the Mississippi, a freshwater drainage system hundreds of millions of years old.

Plans for Lock and Dam 26's river museum include exhibits on ecology; the master plan for the area affected by the new construction includes an eight hundred-acre "environmental demonstration area" on the Missouri bank just below the dam. Wetlands and prairie habitats will be created here, along with recreational facilities. The hope is that man-made nature can compensate for the nature man has disturbed.

Alton, a nineteenth-century city that long rivaled St. Louis, begins a mile upriver on Illinois 143. Cross East Broadway at the stoplight and continue up Ridge two short blocks. Turn right on Fourth, along which are several nineteenth-century stone, frame, and brick houses. A left on Monument provides a postcard view of the angel-topped column Alton constructed as a memorial to Elijah Lovejoy.

Alton's interesting topography and architecture make the city a very pleasant place. Yet its history has a bitter edge. The monument commemorates a brutal incident that occurred the very year of the city's incorporation.

Young Elijah Lovejoy, a Presbyterian minister and newspaper editor, had a passionate devotion to freedom. His aim as a journalist was to present "Truth in all its severity." As a Christian, and as a Maine Yankee bred to abhor human bondage, he had no doubts about the south's peculiar institution. "Slavery is wrong."

After he had seen a black man burned to death in St. Louis, his campaign for slavery's abolition grew so ferocious that he had to leave town. But Alton's many Southern sympathizers were even less tolerant of him than St. Louisans had been. They threw three of his printing presses into the river. He and his supporters were defending a fourth press when a mob set fire to the warehouse where it was stored. Lovejoy climbed to the roof to put out the fire; someone shot him with a double-barreled shotgun.

The memorial was put up by a penitent "Alton that slew him" in 1897 to remind us that it was also "Alton that defended him."

Make a left on Fifth and, three blocks after the late Art Deco St. Clare's Hospital, a right on Henry into the Middletown Historic District. Alton has three such districts, sign of a well-developed sense of its own history. At 1105 Henry is the Federal-style Lyman Trumbull House. He wrote the 13th amendment to the Constitution which abolished slavery. Just beyond, at 1211 Henry, is the Haskell Playhouse — a bit of Victorian froth. One of Alton's many well-kept parks stretches behind it.

A right on 15th and then a left on Liberty take you past a number of handsome houses with fine porches. The scale here is modern: not too big, not too small, not too opulent. One block after Euclid turn right on Grove and right again on Central. Follow Central's curves back to East Broadway, which parallels the river, and turn right.

Veer left at the fork in the road occupied by a wedge-shaped brick building. The feel in Alton's business district is quite different from genteel Henry Street. Alton is still, as evidenced by the busy river, a working town.

At 123 East Broadway is the Alton Museum of History and Art, housed in a couple of nineteenth-century buildings on Antique Row. Exhibits range from memorabilia of the world's tallest man, Robert Wadlow, to displays about Alton's economic history — steamboats, flour mills, glassworks, and railroads. There's also a Lincoln room and a Lovejoy printshop. In the lobby of the neighboring Alton Telegraph a section of the press Lovejoy died defending is on display.

Just before Piasa Street is a stone reminder that here took place the last of the Lincoln-Douglas debates, which led Lincoln to the White House. The marker shares its quasi-piazza with a bus stop, a parking lot, and a visitors center where you may pick up a map. Before turning right on Piasa, look at the grain silos north on East Broadway: white, grey, and brick red, they form a gateway over the road.

Go left on Third Street through Alton's shopping street. Turn right on State and head uphill through a stretch of freshly painted brick and frame houses. This is the Christian Hill Historic District. After Olin Park, turn left at State's T intersection with Ninth Street.

Across from the public school stadium, a left on Danforth Street takes you into Fairmont, this area's answer to St. Louis' private places. Wind on Danforth through woods and past river views, best in winter, to no. 70, an elegant stone house. Curve around it and Danforth becomes Logan, which takes you out of Fairmont's staid elegance and back to State. Turn left there and right two blocks later on Mitchell. This takes you past an orderly housing project. Turn right on Belle (U.S. 67), which dips up and down through woods and takes you back to Alton's downtown.

Turn right on Fourth, cross State and take the first left down Williams Street. Here stands a fragment of the old Alton prison, where thousands of Confederate prisoners died of unconscionable overcrowding and hygienic neglect.

Turn right on River Road, noting the river framed by the mills.

Alton Lake appears on the left; on the right is parking for the thirteen-mile bike path up to Grafton. With its bluffs, trees and sailboats, the scene is almost glamorous.

Two miles up the river is the recently repainted Piasa Bird. The first European to see its image here was Marquette, in 1673. Legend has it that this monstrous bird with a taste for human flesh terrorized Illini Indians until a heroic chief cleverly encompassed its death. The image high on the bluff commemorates that victory.

Eight and a half miles upstream turn right into the Village of Elsah. The street, after winding past many of the village's nineteenth-century stone houses, reaches a stop sign. Turn right up the hill to The Principia College.

At the top of the hill, a security guard will give you a map of the campus. For best use of the fifteen minutes of car travel allowed, veer right after the tennis courts and field house. At the first stop sign, cross over and wind behind the 1930s' Bernard Maybeck buildings to the parking lot behind the chapel. The view from the bluff is wonderful. So are Maybeck's buildings, even from behind. As you return, a right at the tennis court will reveal their fronts.

Maybeck modeled the campus loosely on an English village, an informality reflecting his gently eccentric character. A Californian trained by the same Paris teacher as H. H. Richardson, he liked to use materials both honestly and creatively. Notice the carefully crafted but raw concrete in between these buildings' Tudor half-timbers. Well-known preservationist Charles Hosmer, who teaches on campus, also points out Maybeck's weeping mortar, laid on "as though a grocer had done it."[1] This was one of the architect's ways of avoiding an institutional uptightness. You can best appreciate Maybeck's genius, however, by visiting the buildings' interiors; *that* can be arranged in advance by calling the college's hospitality office.

Exit the campus and turn left. If Principia is like an English village, intact Elsah, the first entire community to be listed on the National Register of Historic Places, is the prime example of a Mississippi River hamlet. At the bottom of the hill either turn right to see Elsah in your car or cross the street to the visitor's parking lot and stroll. Established in the 1840s as a cordwood station for steamboats, Elsah was bought in the following decade by General James Semple, former chargé d'affaires at Bogota. Semple offered a town lot to anyone who would build a stone house on it — one reason for the village's solidity.

Note the Village of Elsah Museum in an 1857 school at Alma and Mill. After you've crossed three bridges over Askew Creek, turn around at Cemetery Road.

As you backtrack, turn right at the Elsah Museum and cross the bridge to the white frame Methodist Church. Veer left onto Lasalle past the carefully contextual Christian Science church. Beyond is the Elsah Village Hall, crowned with a belfry, and Elsah's Landing, whose pies and soups you will enjoy if you don't mind waiting in line.

Brussels Ferry

Back on River Road, go right past Chatauqua, with its old lighthouse near the entrance. Beyond is Grafton, where the Illinois enters the Mississippi.

Just beyond the town appear the stone Pere Marquette Department of Corrections building and a rock outcropping crowned by a cross where Marquette and Joliet landed, or so it is conjectured. Farther north is the Brussels ferry landing. Here you can cross the Illinois for Calhoun County.

Just before the lodge entrance to Pere Marquette State Park, look on the right for the 1876 Hartford Methodist Church, remnant of the town which once stood on the park grounds.

Pere Marquette's visitors center is to the left of the lodge entrance road. A right takes you to the CCC-built lodge, which has a grand log interior. Recent renovation has encouraged crowds; on fine weekend days there is a long wait at the restaurant.

The park's eight thousand acres make it Illinois' largest. Of its numerous attractions you should not miss the scenic drive, which begins between the lodge and the visitors center and ascends the bluffs. The best of the overlooks, two miles beyond the lodge, is up a cedar-lined ramp to the right of the road. From here you glimpse Gilbert Lake, the Illinois, and the Mississippi.

During your descent back to the River Road, note the yellowish soil exposed in banks along the drive. This is loess. When the last glaciers retreated, gales clashing with prevailing winds produced violent dust storms. This dust — really fine soil — settled on bluff tops. Under some conditions, as here, it supports forests. But when exposed to wind and sun, as on bluffs facing south and west, it creates a hill prairie environment.

Return to the River Road and head right. At 5.5 miles, turn left into the Glades River Access, half-gravel, half-paved. The road winds through swampy terrain to Coon Creek Road. Here we have an example of the placid funk of midwestern riparian culture: houses on stilts in various shapes and states, with names like Pauper's Den, Budweiser Geyser, Moon Light Madness, and Rowdy River Rats. Huge shade trees mean that light is mostly reflected from the river.

Back on River Road turn left. The floodplain here supports many prosperous farms.

Cross the Illinois on the bridge at Hardin. Turn right (north). After a little over a mile you will see a large sign on the right for the Barefoot Inn Bar. It's a *way* down home place where boaters and bikers go with families to eat fried catfish and chicken. There is a "Corn from Around the World" display behind the homemade fudge counter.

Continue north on Illinois 100. Just outside Michael, opposite Apple Kingdom Antiques, is a white nineteenth-century river pilot's house moved via barge from Hannibal.

Ten miles to the north is Kampsville. This small town is center of an important archaeological effort conducted by Northwestern University. The digs, which have yielded much information about life here nine thousand years ago, are visible only in the summer. The excellent small museum remains open from May through October. Displays include mother-of-pearl lures and bone fishhooks, as well as hunting equipment. We also learn that the paleo-Indians gave dogs an honored burial, perhaps for their role in the hunt. There is also Dr. Debbie Debris' amusing hypothesis of what excavations of our consumer society might look like in the distant future.

Backtrack to Hardin, where you will continue south on Local Highway 1 toward Brussels. The road often follows the bluffs which shelter several attractive farm-steads. The trees sometimes host bald eagles.

Isolated Calhoun County's charms multiply as you continue south. Twenty miles from Hardin Local 1 turns left. Note the double-galleried brick house at the cross-road. Brussels begins not long after the turn. At the next stop a formless plaza opens; on your left there is a plain white frame store, with an unusual early baroque pediment in shingle. On the right side of the square stand a nicely detailed church and rectory. Beyond look for gingerbread trim on both sides of the road; the turreted double porch on the left is one of a kind. The 1847 Wittmond Hotel stands a few yards farther on.

A mile beyond you are faced with a choice of ferries, both about six miles distant. Continue on Local 1 for the no-charge Brussels ferry to Grafton, from whence you can return to St. Louis via Alton.

For the more exotic choice follow signs to the Golden Eagle Ferry, whose paddlewheel transports you across the Mississippi. This seeming anachronism, built in 1928, is in fact more efficient than propellers. The Golden Eagle operates during daylight hours every day between March and mid-December, as well as on fine days during the winter. If you opt for the Golden Eagle, you'll land in Missouri. Follow a gravel drive over a mile to B. A left turn here takes you almost seven miles to Missouri 94. Turn right on Missouri 94 for St. Charles to return to St. Louis via Interstate 70.

For information call:
Alton Museum of History and Art 618-462-2763
Kampsville Archaeological Center 618-653-4316
Kampsville Archaeological Center Museum 618-653-4511
Pere Marquette State Park 618-786-3323
The Principia College 618-374-2131
The Village of Elsah Museum 618-374-1059

Grant's Cabin

Begins at South Broadway entrance to Jefferson Barracks

The fairly dense suburban environment of south St. Louis
County is dotted with surprising natural and cultural
oases. Several of these have intriguing associations with
Ulysses S. Grant, America's greatest general. Beginning
at Jefferson Barracks and ending at Laumeier Sculpture
Park, with Lone Elk as a coda, this tour also suggests
the range and excellence of the county park system.

Commerce dictated St. Louis' site; its position on the
inland waterway system was picked to facilitate its
French founders' trade. But as the United States grew
after the Louisiana Purchase, the city came to have a
military role as well. Fort Bellefontaine, built in 1805
near the confluence of the Mississippi and the Missouri
rivers, first fulfilled this function.

But by the 1820s the army needed something better.
The village of Carondelet, seeing soldiers as a ready
market for its produce, offered to deed the federal government 1702 acres of its common fields for a military
post. That led, in 1826, to the establishment of Jefferson
Barracks. The post soon became the main training,
mustering, and staging ground for the Army of the West.

In 1829 troops from Jefferson Barracks began protecting merchant caravans traveling on the Santa Fe and
other trails, an activity vital to St. Louis' role as the
Metropolis of the West. Jefferson Barracks' soldiers also
"pacified" Indians in the Black Hawk and Seminole

Wars; Black Hawk himself was imprisoned here in 1832. By the time of the Mexican War in the 1840s this had become the biggest army post in the nation.

Jefferson Barracks' functions varied in the century that followed. St. Louis benefactors, led by Washington University's William G. Eliot, turned it into one of the nation's largest and most efficient hospitals during the Civil War; later the post became a cavalry training center. In this century it was site both of the first successful parachute jump, in 1912, and, in the 1930s, of a Civilian Conservation Corps camp. During World War II, along with other uses, it served as a detention center for Axis prisoners of war. In 1946 it was evacuated by regular U.S. forces. Beginning in 1950 the county acquired 423 acres for the park here today.

The park's entrance is at the end of South Broadway a few blocks beyond the St. Louis city limits. Inside the park Broadway becomes Grant. A sign on the left will lead you to the 1851 Laborers' House, which can be toured, as well as to the stone stables and Visitor Center. A short drive or pleasant walk beyond is the Old Ordnance Room, used for exhibitions, and, some yards south, the Powder Magazine, built in 1857.

All these buildings, especially the Ordnance Room and the Powder Magazine, are worth seeing even if they are closed, as they are Mondays, Tuesdays, and Januarys. Something about the site invites meditation — and it is not simply the old post's manifold historical associations, nor the view of the broad river from the plaza adjacent to the Powder Room. The buildings themselves have a compelling air of finality about them. Unadorned within their stone enclosures, the thick, low, nearly windowless structures are powerfully monumental.

The Powder Magazine contains an old-fashioned but interesting museum which suggests the richness of the post's history. Robert E. Lee and Jefferson Davis both served here; the latter was the officer entrusted with accompanying Black Hawk to the Barracks. George Catlin painted the noble Indian leader's portrait, and Washington Irving interviewed him here. Irving's reaction suggests the moral perplexities nation-building engendered: ". . . I find it extremely difficult, even when near the seat of the action, to get at the right story . . . between the white man and the red man. And my sympathies are strongly with the latter."[1]

Ulysses S. Grant, who came to the Barracks fresh out of West Point in 1843, also had some perplexities about what the army post represented. First of all, as he put it in his memoirs, "A military life had no charms for me . . . ." He had consented to go to West Point from his native Ohio because the trip there would enable him to see Philadelphia and New York. "I had not the faintest idea of staying in the army," he added, even if he did graduate, which he did not expect to do.[2]

Though Grant distinguished himself in the Mexican War, he thought it was "one of the most unjust ever waged by a stronger against a weaker nation."[3] And this injustice had an awful consequence. "The Southern rebellion was largely the outgrowth of the Mexican War. Nations, like individuals, are punished for their transgressions. We got our punishment in the most sanguinary and expensive war of modern times."[4] This attitude toward the "unholy" Civil War is the more remarkable since he was that conflict's undisputed hero.

One of the Powder Magazine Museum's exhibits shows Grant considering an invitation to White Haven, nearby home of a West Point classmate's family. His relation to that place was also paradoxical, as we shall see.

Follow Grant Road south (left) through the park. Note

the gateposts at the scenic overlook on the road: four cannons placed bolt upright, a style perhaps inspired by Les Invalides in Paris. Across the parade ground before you 1890s brick barracks with gallery porches are aligned in another of the park's handsome monumental images.

Turn right on Hancock where, just beyond the curve, are former officers' houses, one of which houses a museum dedicated to the Civilian Conservation Corps. The CCC was responsible for the lodges at Illinois' Pere Marquette and Missouri's Washington state parks, among other 1930s environmental projects.

Turn left on Worth and right on Sherman, which after a short distance becomes Jefferson Barracks Road. Turn right onto Telegraph Road and bear right on Kingston, where the neatly sited and maintained brick houses are as orderly as anything on the army post. There is a fine view of St. Louis from the top of the hill here. Kingston meets Broadway near the north entrance of Jefferson Barracks. Turn left and follow Broadway north through Lemay.

The industrial landscape near the Des Peres River includes the Metropolitan Sewer District, Carondelet Coke, and St. Louis Ship plants. The county is planning a port expansion here.

Jesuit fathers, who left Cahokia at the behest of rival priests sent by the bishop of Quebec, established a short-lived mission at the mouth of the Des Peres in 1700, giving what was to become St. Louis its first European settlers, and the river its name. They followed their converts when the Indians crossed the river, founding Kaskaskia.

Continue across the Des Peres into Carondelet. Turn left at Marceau and left again at the first stoplight (Alabama) to recross the Des Peres. Turn right on Weber, which follows the river. Weber becomes first Carondelet

Boulevard and then Des Peres Boulevard. Follow the river for 2.2 miles and turn left on Gravois, then right on Seibert, which quickly becomes Heege. At the bottom of the hill turn right on Genesta and then left on Seth.

Here is Oakland, the country seat of Louis A. Benoist, an immensely successful banker of French-Canadian ancestry. Built in the Italianate style in the mid-1850s, it is the best-preserved work of English architect George I. Barnett, who also did Tower Grove and a number of other St. Louis buildings, as well as Blair House in Washington. Its self-assurance, clarity, and generous proportions are in striking contrast with bland Affton. But it is that community's active historical society which has beautifully restored the house and which offers tours the third Sunday of each month.

Along with many Benoist family pieces within is a somber dining room installed by Washington University benefactor Robert Brookings, who lived here toward the end of the nineteenth century.

Francophiles may choose to concentrate on a document hung high up in the music alcove. Dated 1706, it is a letter to Antoine Benoist, one of Louis XIV's favorite portraitists. Antoine's father, an orphan, had lost his noble titles and privileges as a result of having done manual labor in his youth. This letter, signed by Louis XIV, reinstates the Benoist family as nobles. Finding Louis XIV in Oakland is as much of a surprise as finding Oakland itself in Affton.

Back at Heege turn right, and right again on Mackenzie. As you approach Watson Road, note, to the left, the unusual 1931 domed tower of Cardinal Glennon College.

Turn left on Watson Road, part of the legendary U.S. Route 66. Among that road's most appealing artifacts is the Coral Court Motel at 7755 Watson. See how the 1941 tourist cabin facades glide around glazed tile and glass block corners. Note the screens over the vents, the lamp standards, the Coral Court sign itself. Compare the scale, finish and sheen of this Streamline Moderne complex to more recent highway architecture. It is the motel's easy relation between style and function that inspires nostalgia.

Continue west on Watson and turn left on Laclede Station Road. A block after you cross Rock Hill Road, turn right on White Haven. You have entered Grantwood Village, a well-off, well-tended community of brick ranch houses, built on what was once the estate of Grant's wife's family. At 9060, near the end of the road, you will see White Haven with its fine gallery porches. The nine-acre plot now belongs to the National Park Service, which plans to open the property to the public in due time. Built in 1818 by W. L. Long for his wife Elizabeth Sappington, it became the property of Frederick Dent in 1820, and, after the Civil War, of Grant himself, who hoped to retire here after his terms in the White House.

Dent, son of an old Maryland family, had done well as a merchant in Pittsburgh. But he preferred the plantation life; when Grant first visited White Haven his future father-in-law owned eighteen slaves.

The young officer was against slavery. But manners, not to mention his friendship for Colonel Dent's son, and soon a stronger feeling for the planter's eldest daughter, Julia, encouraged Ulysses to keep his opinions quiet. Despite her father's conviction that the military life would not suit her, Grant was able to win Julia's hand.

Military life turned out not to suit Ulysses. After the Mexican War he was stationed in California, where Gold Rush prices made it impossible for him to send for his family. By 1854 he could no longer bear being without his beloved Julia and their two small children. Resigning from the army, he returned to St. Louis to take up farming.

He had high hopes for success, especially after they were able to move to a place of their own, a log cabin he built with his own hands. The site was land Dent had given his daughter a little to the north of White Haven.

On December 28, 1856, a few months after they had moved, he wrote his father, "Evry day I like farming better and I do not doubt but that money is to be made at it . . . My intention is to raise about twenty acres of Irish potatoes, on new ground, five acres of sweet potatoes, about the same of early corn, five or six acres of cabbage, beets, cucumber pickles, mellons and keep a wagon going to market evry day."[5]

But by February 7, 1857, he was less sanguine. His funds were so low that he had to haul wood to provide his family the bare necessities. This did not seem undignified to him. When an old companion at arms who came upon him with his wagonload of wood exclaimed, "Great God, Grant, what are you doing?" Grant replied, "I am solving the problem of poverty."[6]

But he wasn't. Before long he had to abandon farming. Real estate in St. Louis, his next venture, did not turn out any better. Perhaps he lacked the stuff of a businessman; in the spring of 1859 he freed, rather than sold, a slave he had bought from his father-in-law.

In August he applied for the position of county engineer. Despite recommendations from such solid citizens as Oakland's Louis Benoist and Taylor Blow, the commissioners rejected him. Discouraged, he told his father that he would not even try for a post as mathematics professor at Washington University, though it was "one of the best endowed institutions in the United States."[7]

He had come from a successful family and had married into a successful family. But he was a failure. In early 1860, he moved with his family to Galena, Illinois, to take up work in his father's leather business.

Had the St. Louis experience been in vain? Civil War historian Bruce Catton thinks not: "A character was built in that time." Self-mastery learned here made him master of others in the conflict that was to come.[8]

Backtrack on Whitehaven Road to Laclede Station and turn right. Turn right again on Gravois, which takes you across Gravois Creek, past the bronze harts of the Busch estate entrance and finally to Grant's cabin. There is now an ornate gate in front.

Irony must have helped Grant in the lean years. His wife's father had named White Haven after the Dents' ancestral seat in Maryland, theirs since the seventeenth

Laumier Sculpture Park

century. Ulysses dubbed his own place "Hardscrabble."

That was not enough. Even though Grant had built it with his own hands, the nicely proportioned dwelling did not suit Mrs Grant; not many months passed before the family was back at White Haven.

Hardscrabble stands in interesting juxtaposition with the Busches' sumptuous 1911 red-roofed castle, which you glimpse from Gravois. It's difficult to imagine what Grant would have made of the grandeur. A consummate horseman and teamster himself, he certainly would have appreciated the Clydesdales, sometimes visible here along with a rich menagerie.

At the corner of the Busch grounds, turn right on Eddie and Park and right again on Pardee. Note the 1820 Long Cabin at the corner of Pardee Spur and Pardee. It was built by the original owner of White Haven, W.L. Long. Follow Pardee left along Gravois Creek, where you'll pass White Cliff Park, home of the Crestwood Community Center. Turn left on Grant and left again on Watson by Crestwood Plaza. Just beyond the shopping center turn right on New Sappington Road, which takes you to the Sappington House, a circa 1808 brick structure on the left as interesting as it is beautiful. Turn left onto its grounds, complete with tidy outbuildings and garden. There is also a tea room here, as well as a pond and a library of Americana and decorative arts.

Return to Watson and head right 1.7 miles for Laumeier Sculpture Park. Turn left just before Watson's intersection with 270. Turn left quickly again on Rott Road. The entrance to Laumeier is a few yards down Rott on your right. The house and land were given to St. Louis County by Mrs. Laumeier in 1968. Sculptor Ernest Trova donated a number of his works as nucleus of an outdoor sculpture collection, and the park opened in

1976. Laumeier is enjoyable both for the growing collection and for the way it's presented.

Too often museums discourage spontaneity; at Laumeier the solemn ritual of Art Appreciation has been sabotaged. Sculpture's relation to the outdoors — not to mention dogs, joggers, barbecues, and frisbees — is more than sufficient to restore a visitor's sense of marvel.

The indoor gallery also has lively exhibitions. Near its entrance you will find a map, essential for a thorough visit to the park's riches. If you don't have a specific target, you might begin with the north lawn near Rott. Here a brash di Suvero contrasts with a Richard Fleischner rock installation which creates a perspective from the park to the office complex across Rott. Embedded in the drive to the front of the house is a Richard Serra circle. On the lawn nearby is a George Rickey wind sculpture whose steel needles move fluidly as sea anemones.

As you return to the gallery side of the house, note the careful crafting of the stainless steel Trova at the northwest corner. Proceed now along the axis of the park's largest meadow for the 12 bold red cylinders assembled by Alex Liberman. The adjacent meadow, just to the right, holds, among other works, Beverly Pepper's orange *Alpha* and Donald Judd's three minimalist boxes.

Return toward the house, noting the flattened white boat hull of Robert Stackhouse's *St. Louie Bones* between it and the outdoor stage.

Many of the park's most characteristic works are in its tree-covered northeast quadrant. Along a trail which begins behind the stage, you will discover sculptures in earth and wood, each created for its particular woodland site. As such works "would be destroyed physically or ideologically, or both, by removal," they are described as site specific.[9] Laumeier's is the United States' most ambitious site specific program.

This tour has been a series of surprises: history in a park at Jefferson Barracks, a grand villa in the bland suburb of Affton, a Louis XIV autograph in a music room, a real log cabin next to an almost real chateau, elaborate works of art hidden in the west county woods. If Laumeier's peculiarity is that of art in nature, that of the tour's finale, Lone Elk Park, is nature in nature, or to be precise, the fauna in the flora.

Return to Watson Road and go west on Interstate 44. After 4.4 miles, take exit 272. At the end of the exit ramp turn right on Missouri 141 and immediately right onto another ramp which takes you to North Outer Road. Turn left. Lone Elk is at the end of Outer Road.

Herds of bison, elk, fallow deer, Barbados sheep, geese and wild turkeys share the 405-acre county park. They can be seen along a well-marked auto tour. The park's Raptor Center likewise affords a close-up view of birds of prey.

Lone Elk may have a companion park across I-44, where plans to purchase a large tract of undeveloped forest are underway.

You may return to St. Louis by I-44.

For information call:
Grant's Farm Tours 843-1700
Jefferson Barracks 544-5714
Laumeier Sculpture Park 821-1209
Lone Elk Park 225-4390
Oakland House 352-5654
Raptor Center 225-4390
Sappington House 957-4785

Kirkwood depot

Begins at Big Bend and Old Orchard in Webster Groves

America's first settlers crossed the sea to escape Old World obstacles to their material ambitions or spiritual goals. Ruthless pursuit of their ends made some, like La Salle, the embodiment of Machiavelli's Prince. Others, like most missionaries and reformers, saw the New World as a possible Utopia. They came to build a society reflecting that vision.

This double heritage accounts for some of the peculiarities of the United States today. Americans did not want to impose restraints on the economic activity that was making so many of them rich. Our cities, with industry's growth in the nineteenth century, consequently became chaotic and polluted. Immigrant laborers, fodder for the factories, added social confusion to environmental disorder.

But capitalists, unwilling to regulate their sooty yet profitable enterprises, were also unwilling to renounce their ideals of the good life. America's spaciousness afforded them a sort of resolution to this conflict. At the same time, American tradition justified what might otherwise have appeared a massive evasion of civic responsibility.

Daniel Boone's dislike of crowds had become as much a legend as his wilderness savvy. Thomas Jefferson, hardly a backwoodsman, shared the dislike and considered cities "pestilential to the morals, the health, and the liberties of man."[1] Two generations later Calvert Vaux declared that the move away from the city showed nothing less than "a preference for the works of God to the works of man."[2]

Such anti-urban views found ready listeners. In 1849 St. Louis was devastated by both a catastrophic fire and a cholera epidemic. That gave urgency to rich St. Louisans' attempts to improve their environment, attempts that included platting private streets, whose deed restrictions and covenants managed to eliminate some urban nuisances, much as zoning at the municipal level does today.

The coming of the railroad in mid-century offered a more drastic solution. Improvements like the private places were piecemeal; why not take the train out of the city altogether? Commuter service meant people could have their cake and eat it too.

"In 1911," the *History of St. Louis County* explains, "two thousand men of Webster Groves make life pleasant by living there and profitable by the conduct of business in St. Louis." Rail service had fathered Webster in the mid-nineteenth century. At its peak twenty-seven trains ran "each way, each day." Six depots served as many sections of a town that "has no factories or saloons; not that these naturally come or go together, but the city doesn't want either of them."[3]

Our tour begins at Big Bend, so called for the trail the Indians took to the 'big bend' of the Meramec River, and Old Orchard, named for the first of two orchards early settler Richard Lockwood planted here. The large new Orchard House complex at this almost urban intersection has retirement apartments, shops, and offices.

A number of cultural institutions also give Webster a citified air. Go west on Big Bend. Near its intersection with Lockwood, on the left, is Nerinx Hall, a girls' high school. The central portion of the school is Lockwood's house, all but hidden by additions.

Webster University, established here in 1916, is down Big Bend. Across from Bompart Avenue is the Tudor-style Music Department. Beyond its pleasant lawn is the

Loretto-Hilton Theater, home of both the St. Louis
Repertory Theatre and of Opera Theatre of St. Louis.

Like the St. Louis Symphony, whose members play
at its performances, Opera Theatre has become a
national treasure. Founded in 1976, it presents a program of classics, neglected masterpieces, and contemporary works, all sung in English by young American
performers.

Continuing on Big Bend take the first right,
Plymouth. From the corner of Lockwood and
Plymouth, Eden Seminary is visible. Founded in
Marthasville in 1850 by German Evangelicals, the
seminary moved here in 1925.

Turn left on Lockwood, then right on Joy. This
enclave, Webster Park, exemplifies much of nineteenth-
century suburban theory. Notice the curved roadways.
Earlier town planning was almost always based on the
grid; right angles asserted man's dominance over
nature. The nineteenth century's taming of the wilderness meant that it could now be idealized. Once terror
no longer lurked there, people wanted a closer relation
with nature. Broad setbacks, apparently spontaneous
groupings of trees and bushes, and open lawns completed a vision most convincingly realized in the United
States by Frederick Law Olmsted, Calvert Vaux's
partner.

Note at 30 Joy the shingled carriage house. At the
circle, turn right on Oakwood which you follow to
Park. A left on Park and a left on Hawthorne bring you
past 410, a stone and frame carriage house. Turn right
on Orchard to 405 (on the left) an unassuming gray and
white structure that was Webster Park's first house.
Turn around, then turn right on Hawthorne, and left on
Glen. Go left on Oakwood, which you follow to Mason.
Turn right; at 40 Mason is a fine Greek Revival house.

Turn right on Lockwood and left at City Hall on
South Elm, where recent rehabs and new houses have
maintained the Victorian frame tradition. A right on

Oak Terrace — 1920s bungalows — and a right again on South Gore will show you more residential Victoriana.

At Lockwood turn left past the well-stocked Webster Groves Bookshop and right on North Gore, a shopping street established here for its vicinity to the train depot. Just before the railroad tracks turn right into the parking lot of the recycled Missouri Pacific station, served by commuter trains until 1961.

Backtrack to Lockwood and turn right. Turn left one block on Gray. Note no. 133's peculiar porch. Go right on Jackson, then left on South Rock Hill Road.

Beyond I-44 and Big Bend are the Reavis Place Hawken condominiums, advertised as "traditional Webster Groves Victorian architecture." The frame style, with fish scale shingles and sociable porches, is in tune with the town, but the deep lawns and impressive groves are lacking. Just beyond is the 1857 Hawken House, built by one of the rifle-making family. The Webster Groves Historical Society opens the house to visitors.

Backtrack on Rock Hill, crossing Big Bend and I-44. Just beyond the tracks turn left on Frisco and right on Sherwood, which runs through another typically spacious Webster neighborhood, this one with magnificent trees. Go left on Lockwood, which, after a jog left on Berry Road, leads west into Glendale.

Five blocks west of Berry Road turn right on Edwin Avenue: at 115 stands a handsome 1859 brick house with a double gallery porch, built for William McPherson, president of the Missouri Pacific. Continue north to Essex where a left will take you into Kirkwood, named after the Missouri Pacific's chief engineer at the time of its founding in the 1850s. The site includes the highest point on the line between St. Louis and Jefferson City, which gave the town a reputation as a healthful place.

Like Webster Groves, Kirkwood maintained a high tone. "The moral atmosphere of Kirkwood is clear," *The Suburban Leader* assured readers on December 18, 1895.

"No saloons are allowed in town and the entire community is singularly free from vicious resorts or evil allurements for the young."[4]

Just after the city limits turn left on Dickson — there's a stop sign. Head south several blocks to Argonne, where, turning right, you see at 549 the Kirkwood History House, home of the Kirkwood Historical Society. Its period rooms are open weekends.

Opposite the History House turn left on Clark and then right on Monroe, where, at 503, is the exuberant green on cream Seven Gables. Across Woodlawn at 217 is a placid white brick house built in 1862. Go right on Woodlawn to Argonne, where, from the corner, you can glimpse 116 North Woodlawn; its daiquiri-colored wood is modeled after Italian stone structures. Turn left on Argonne.

Here you have a typical Kirkwood streetscape, varied and welcoming, yet not without high aspirations. Note, for instance, 440's antebellum Greek Revival facade, or 419's Italianate cornice and windows. At Taylor look to the left for the 1860 Gothic Revival Eliot Chapel.

Turn right on Taylor and right on Adams, where at 217 is a house whose 1859 neo-Gothic trim survives. Turn left into semicircular Douglass Lane to see an 1870 frame house at number 10 — formerly on a three acre lot. Go right on Adams, backtracking to Taylor where you will turn right again. Follow this pleasant street north to Essex. Turn left.

Cross Kirkwood Road on Essex and follow it to Harrison, where you turn left. At 434 Harrison is a noble white brick house dating from the 1860s. Three and a half blocks farther south, at 302 W. Argonne, is the impressive but dilapidated Civil War era Mudd's Grove.

Continue on Harrison over the railway tracks. At the corner of Harrison and Monroe is the immaculate Olive Chapel, the most affecting public structure in Kirkwood. Built for a German congregation in 1896, it was later

National Museum of Transport

bought by the African Methodist Episcopal Church whose Kirkwood history dates back to 1853.

Turn left on Monroe, generously endowed with antique stores. Note at 115 the simple brick Bopp House. Turn left on Kirkwood. Note the mall complex to the east. One of the ways Kirkwood differs from Webster Groves is that the small town scale and feeling has been violated here and at other points on this road. City Hall is to your left. Turn left on Madison, right on Clay and right again on Argonne — here named Old Main Street. Note the Coulter Feed Company advertisement painted on a wall on the left. On the right stands the 1893 Richardsonian Romanesque train station, still in use. Kirkwood has had continuous rail service since 1853. The station is literally the center of Kirkwood; street numbers are calculated from here.

To see a fine collection drawn from the trains that played so strong a role in American history, turn right on Kirkwood and, after a mile, right on Big Bend. Go west 2.7 miles, then turn right on Barrett Station Road. A half mile beyond is the National Museum of Transport. The museum, part of the St. Louis County Park system, includes a display of a number of automobiles, as well as a boat and an airplane.

For information call:
Hawken House 968-1857
Kirkwood History House 965-5151
National Museum of Transport 965-7998

The Church of the Abbey of Saint Mary and Saint Louis

Begins at the Galleria on Clayton Road and Brentwood

In our communal living arrangements we Americans
have tended to solve problems by running away from
them. During the latter part of the nineteenth century
railroads served as escape routes from city soot and
confusion. Yet the suburbs, shaped by railroads, had
much in common with cities, sharing such elements of
sociability and urbanity as sidewalks, porches, and di-
versified shopping districts, as well as heterogeneous
populations.

What made America a suburban nation was not the
railroad, but the automobile. The difference in the two
modes of transportation tells in the communities they
created. Cars encapsulate individuals, usually keeping
them apart; trains brought them together. Lewis Mumford's description of suburbia as a paradoxical "collective
effort to live a private life"[1] is far more applicable to
today's automobile suburbs than to their predecessors.

Ladue, Frontenac, and Town and Country, according
to a recent survey America's fourth, twelfth, and thirty-
eighth richest communities, grew up along U.S. 40 and
Clayton Road. Just east of Ladue is the vastly successful
Galleria.

The United States' earliest car-oriented shopping
center was built on the other side of Missouri, the 1923
Country Club Plaza in Kansas City. But not till the fifties
did malls become common. Since then, the now usually
climate-proof centers have become vital not only to
retailing, but also to many people's social lives. Yet like

the suburbs they serve, these controlled environments limit encounters with anyone outside the economic class each targets.

Going west on Clayton you see two ecclesiastical structures, on the left, the Church of the Immacolata, on the right, Harris Armstrong's 1964 copper-roofed Ethical Society, both designed to attract the notice of passing drivers.

Farther west you will see Busch's Grove. Built before the Civil War, this gathering place has been a stagecoach stop, grocery store, post office, and resort hotel, as well as a tavern and restaurant. At the turn of the century Busch's amenities included a lake, not to mention a barnyard with pigs and poultry. The picturesque unpeeled log pavilions are for summer dining. Beyond, also on the left, is another of Ladue's several social institutions, the white-columned Bogey Club, here since 1911.

To the right, beyond the Church of the Annunziata, are Ladue's city buildings. Incorporated in 1936, when farms still existed in the area, the community has been careful to maintain its country air. Note the woodsy tangle on the other side of Clayton Road.

Opposite the Ladue Chapel turn right onto Barnes Road, at the end of which you will see the grounds of the St. Louis Country Club. Its relocation in what was to become Ladue greatly enhanced the desirability of the surrounding area for residential use.

Established with fifteen members in 1892, this most exclusive of St. Louis clubs grew to 250 before the turn of the century. It moved here from its Hanley Road location in Clayton in 1914. The great greensward of its golf course constitutes a rare opening in Ladue's landscape. Rare because Ladue, to a degree found nowhere else in this region, has opted out of the American lawn culture.

America's lawns, which cover 50,000 square miles of the nation, and on which we spend $30 billion a year, puzzle observers.[2] They did not always exist, for one thing; foreigners commented on nineteenth-century

American homesteads' out-of-door slovenliness.

Frederick Law Olmsted changed that. His planned suburbs included houses set back from the street to make space for lawns. These were to remain unfenced, giving the impression of a single vast park. His followers believed "It is unchristian to hedge from the sight of others the beauties of nature which it has been our good fortune to create or secure."[3] In this context it is understandable why someone called the lawn "an institution of democracy," and mowing "a civic responsibility."[4]

Ladue has fine lawns, yet the overall effect is of a landscape of exclusion. How did that happen? Thorstein Veblen, in *The Theory of the Leisure Class*, wrote of upper class Americans' "pseudo return to the primitive" as a reaction to nineteenth-century robber barons' conspicuous consumption.[5] Built mainly in this century, Ladue has chosen to conceal rather than exhibit its wealth. Aside from the reason Veblen suggests, people like the inhabitants of Ladue had no need to advertise; they all knew one another, and to a surprising degree still do. Sidewalks, necessary to sociability elsewhere, here are forbidden. Where they do exist, after a fashion, they are referred to as paths.

Visitors will be pleased or put off by Ladue's exclusiveness. But the manner of it cannot fail to gain the approval of anyone who values living in harmony with nature.

An early and extremely persuasive proponent of that harmony was architect William Bernoudy. A student of Frank Lloyd Wright in the 1930s, Bernoudy designed hundreds of houses in the St. Louis region. Yet he succeeded so well in his wish that they be "embosomed in the landscape,"[6] to use Lewis Mumford's phrase, that very few of them are visible from the road. If you turn around at the country club entrance, you will see — or rather not see — an example at 750 Barnes, cloaked in green most of the year.

Fortunately the 1954 residence at the corner of Barnes

and Upper Barnes, which you may see by turning on Upper Barnes, gives a notion of what magic the integration of art and nature can produce. Its low roofs and wide eaves show its Prairie School parentage; the carefully thought out details, perfect proportions, and delicate relation to the land testify to Bernoudy's finesse. The addition's placement at a right angle to the rest plays down the structure's size, yet maintains the discreetly monumental appeal of the whole.

Return to Clayton, turn right and right again at Warson. On the right, beginning at Old Chatham Road, are grand estates. Turn right on Ladue Road Cut-off and right again on Chateau Oaks. Here most of the houses were built at the end of the 1980s, in styles chosen to hide that fact. Their imperious bearing contrasts dramatically with the earthy manner of the Prairie School.

Back at Ladue Road Cut-off turn right, then left at the stop sign onto Ladue Road. From the corner of Ladue and Warson you may see Mary Institute, a girls' school established by William Greenleaf Eliot, the founder of Washington University. His grandson, T.S. Eliot, who had grown up not far from the school's former city location, returned in 1959 to speak at its 100th anniversary celebration.

Backtrack on Warson and stay on it across Clayton. At Litzsinger Road turn right. Cross Lindbergh and drive to the brand-new Litzsinger Place. Here the exclusion Ladue achieves by landscape is wrought differently.

Back on Lindbergh turn left for the most sumptuous of shopping malls, Plaza Frontenac. Turn left on Clayton Road. Continue a couple of miles west to Geyer Road's stoplight, where you turn left. If the suburbs represent an escape from city soot, street names along Geyer suggest an escape into fantasy. Does Georgian Acres contain Georgian houses? What relation has Outer Ladue Road to Ladue Road or Ladue City? And was Steeplechase Lane ever the site of races?

The 1833 Des Peres Presbyterian Meeting House constitutes a calm rebuke to its surroundings and not just architecturally. "A power for good" in all its history, an early county chronicle assures us, it was "supported for many years by people who traveled, in most cases, magnificent distances to reach the sanctuary."[7] Elijah Lovejoy preached here. Continue south past Coach-n-Four Lane. At the stop just beyond, turn right on Countryside Lane to turn around. Return to Clayton Road; turn left. The next few miles afford glimpses of several Palladian clusters.

Neoclassical display, never a winning mode, reached new heights in the 1980s. Compare these recent constructions to the ranch houses lining most of Clayton Road. These were constructed in the fifties and sixties, when American culture was self-confident. The defeats and economic instability of the seventies and eighties engendered architectural ostentation.

Turn right on Mason Road. A short distance beyond U.S. 40, turn right at the St. Louis Priory School/St. Anselm Parish sign. Priory Chapel's interior, more than the festive exterior, is a meditative antidote to nearby residential pomp. The chapel is a 1962 work of HOK, with Pier Luigi Nervi as consultant.

Backtrack on Mason across U.S. 40/I-64 and Clayton Road. Continue south to Queeny Park. Follow signs for the Dog Museum, housed in the 1853 Jarville. Here, too, the neo-Palladian vocabulary — columns, dentils, a pediment, an ocular window and even two sets of gates — is used. Yet the house appears the embodiment of modesty. Built by Hyacinthe Renard, Pierre Laclede's grandson-in-law, Jarville was remodeled in the 1930s for Edgar Queeny, son of Monsanto's founder.

It now houses the Dog Museum. You may see paintings by one of Louis XV's favorites, Oudry, as well as a room dedicated to mastiffs, or video presentations of different breeds. The Dog Museum, a national institution which moved to St. Louis, has just completed an expansion.

For information call:
Dog Museum 821-3647

Shrine of Our Lady of the Snows

Begins at the Cahokia Mounds, exit 6 off Interstate 55

Most itineraries in this book combine points of interest linked by similarities, or at the very least by arcane harmonies. The claim cannot be made of our final tour.

"Aren't you glad you live in Belleville?" a bank advertisement there asks. This approach would not work in some neighboring towns, where getting out seems the only hope. Yet the east side's history and challenges are instructive. And despite its devastation, much of the area is not without a kind of luster.

We begin, however, with a place of yet another destiny. In the floodplain east of St. Louis a high heap of earth near I-55 surprises some travelers. Others dismiss it, one writer suggests, as "the misbegotten foundation of an unfinished overpass."[1] Even as clever an observer as Charles Dickens, here in 1841, had more to say about the Trappists who gave the place its name, Monks Mound, than about the great pile's meaning. Though this is the largest prehistoric earthen structure in the New World, its chief attraction was the grand view of the St. Louis skyline its summit affords.

Yet St. Louis, "Mound City" before real estate developers razed its two dozen or so elevations, was once a mere satellite of this place. Europeans named the complex Cahokia Mounds — not for the extinct culture that built it half a millennium earlier — but for the unrelated Cahokia tribe that had migrated here not long before the

French arrived. Almost seventy mounds are included in the 2,200-acre state historic site; the United Nation's World Heritage Site boundary encircles well over a hundred.

Turn off I-55 at exit 6. Head right at the end of the ramp and then left on Collinsville Road. Immediately beyond a quarry on the left you see a reconstruction of an A.D. 1000 solar calendar, Woodhenge. As you approach the mounds, going toward the Interpretive Center, you begin to distinguish time and plow softened shapes — platform, ridgetop, conical — reminiscent of ancient structures in what is now Latin America. Cahokia's mound builders may in fact have been in contact with their southern counterparts, for the Cahokians traded widely.

One of the reasons they built their city here was that the nearby meeting of the Illinois, Missouri, and Mississippi rivers gave access to a vast trade territory. Another was that corn, whose culture reached here from Mexico about A.D. 700, grew well. The stable food base made possible a population of twenty or thirty thousand. Cahokia was larger than London in A.D. 1250, and was the largest city North America had seen until Philadelphia surpassed it in 1800.

By that time ancient Cahokia had long since disappeared. What brought about its decline? Climatic change, resource depletion, disease resulting from a corn diet?

Social unrest might well have played a part too. The social order was highly complex; to build the mounds meant disciplining laborers to dig and transport fifty million cubic feet of earth. Who was doing the disciplining?

Excavations of mound 72, not far from the Interpretive Center, suggest the power some individuals had.

Archaeologists uncovered the skeleton of a man about forty-five years old. He was resting on a bed of twenty thousand marine shells, with grave offerings that included eight hundred arrow heads, fifteen chunky game stones, a large pile of mica, a roll of copper. Nearby were found sacrifices: the remains of 4 headless and handless men — and of 118 women between the ages of fifteen and twenty-five.

It is no surprise that palisades were erected within the city, presumably to protect figures such as this man from the lower orders.

In wet seasons near the museum you hear frogs croaking; they are enjoying the waters of the "borrow pits," so called because there clay for the mounds was quarried.

The 1989 museum, located at the eastern edge of the mound complex, is in every way worthy of the site it serves. The handsome structure — notice the bronze doors — contains a cafe and a well-stocked gift shop/ book store. Plan on spending time here; the exhibits are as seductive as they are intelligent. Begin with the multimedia presentation, "City of the Sun," continue with the diorama recreating ancient Cahokia, then browse among the plenteous displays. Along with archaeological and social data are Indian recipes, games, and humorous ceramics like a big toe pipe. The site itself may be visited following paths from the museum or by driving to the Monks Mound and Woodhenge.

Backtrack on Collinsville Road to Illinois 111, which you follow left, south, toward Washington Park. After the melancholy beauty of a great archaeological site, the squalor of East St. Louis' periphery is shocking. The communities we touch on, industry's borrow pits, are counted among America's poorest towns. There is symmetry here; even as Ladue is our fourth richest community, Alorton, which we are skirting as we continue south, is the nation's fourth poorest. East St. Louis is only slightly richer than Alorton, ranked fifth on the poverty scale; adjacent Centreville and Venice, just north, are ninth and eleventh respectively.

Alorton's name hints at its history: it was founded by the Aluminum Ore Company in 1930. By establishing sovereign planned communities, corporations in this area mixed a paternalistic concern for alleviating East St. Louis workers' living conditions, which had been deplorable since the Civil War, with an equally paternalistic desire to control their labor force. In more recent times the original motives have given way to neglect, or, in the case of the Aluminum Ore Company, to abandonment. Alorton's poverty has not broken the pride of the town, whose entrance sign, not visible on this route, assures us that Alorton is "where Jesus Is Lord."

Company towns hereabouts include Granite City, founded in 1895 by the Niedringhaus brothers as home of their steel works, Sauget, originally called Monsanto for its founding company, and National City, the stockyards village. Ringing East St. Louis, these separate municipalities diminished that city's tax base, as the suburbs had reduced St. Louis'.

East St. Louis taxes, though greater than in the company towns, were in any case skewed in favor of corporations. Assessed property valuation was less than half what it was in other Illinois cities of its size. The difference was made up in saloon license fees, a plentiful fount. East St. Louis workers sought solace in drink to an abnormal degree, perhaps because their wages were half what workers in Belleville received.

The numerous railroads serving the city made it easy for corporations to recruit new labor, insuring that wages remained low. One of the most shameful incidents in the area's history resulted from the cut-throat job competition thus induced. In 1917 Aluminum Ore workers went on strike. The First World War had cut off the supply of European immigrants, and poor blacks had taken their places. On July 2 rioters, with police and National Guard acquiescence and even participation, killed at least thirty-nine blacks in cold blood.

St. Louis policemen stationed on Eads Bridge protected the hundreds who fled, and city relief agencies provided food and shelter. This decent behavior provided a counterpoint to the historical fact that St. Louisans had long profited from East St. Louis, whose wealth was overwhelmingly controlled by non-residents.

Despite unfair and even iniquitous circumstances, the east side built up one of the great industrial bases of the world. How could it have declined so drastically?

Its very success created part of the problem. Early-twentieth-century industrial plants are easier to abandon than to fit for new technology. Trucking, favored by the federally funded interstate highway system, hastened railways' decline; the East St. Louis yards were especially inefficient. Civic corruption, labor problems, and crime also induced the departure of some industries.

The 1980s failed to reverse post-war decline. Impressive plans to develop the impressive waterfront fell through, not for lack of funding but for the fecklessness of authorities. Population loss accelerated; arson, crumbling sewers, and stoppage of municipal trash collection now brutalize the city.

Despite perpetual crisis and hopelessness, East St. Louis still achieves excellence, and it does so with a regularity that would make far more privileged communities gleeful. The East St. Louis High School Flyers repeatedly play — and win — the Illinois state football championship; in 1985 *USA Today* named them best team in the nation. Lincoln High basketball players likewise triumph in their sport. That school's girls track team, of which Jackie Joyner-Kersee, Olympic gold medal winner, is a graduate, also dominates state meets.

Success is not limited to sports. The Lincoln High Jazz Band won a national championship in 1987, and was invited to play at jazz festivals both in Montreux and The Hague. These performers are in a long line of renowned East St. Louis artists; best known is dancer Katherine Dunham, to whom a museum is dedicated here. The city's successes artistically and athletically suggest what rich human capital the otherwise drained East St. Louis might draw on.

Illinois 111 ends at a state park; turn left on Lake Drive, then right on Illinois 157. Soon thereafter a turn left (east) on Illinois 15 takes you up the bluff above the floodplain and almost at once to the Shrine of Our Lady of the Snows.

Of the shrines mentioned in the course of these tours, this is by far the most successful. Urban theories hypothesize that some towns' origins lie in religious activities. Our Lady of the Snows, with its new church, motel, restaurant, indoor theater, outdoor amphitheater — constructed of playful concrete parabolas — and retirement community already looks like a neat little city.

The grounds, with the Lourdes Grotto, the Annunciation Garden, the Agony in the Garden, stations of the cross with button-activated messages, and the Resurrection Garden, might put one in mind of a theme park. But they are so spacious and well-tended, such a relief after the bedraggled and degraded scenes down on the plain, that they are restful.

For those who want energy, on the other hand, there is the million-dollar multimedia, multisensory experience, "The Power," shown in the Guild Center. Developed by a consortium of Christian denominations for the 1982 World's Fair in Knoxville, Tennessee, "The Power" packs a gospel punch in twenty-two minutes when "time is suspended," and "the whole cosmic drama is relived."

Activities at the shrine also have a universal range, from concerts to multi-cultural Easter egg displays, from Maronite, American Indian, and Polish American celebrations, to the annual Christmas Way of Lights. The shrine is part of the outreach of the Missionary Oblates of Mary Immaculate, whose many members work on all continents.

Return to Illinois 15 and follow it right (south) to Belleville's Centerville Avenue exit. Turn left on Centerville into town, where you will turn right on Lincoln then right on South Third. Admire St. Elizabeth Hospital's 1951 glass, yellow brick, and stainless steel Soviet deco facade. The hospital was founded by German nuns in 1875.

At the stop sign turn left on Harrison, admiring the very rich, very correct neo-Gothic St. Peter's Cathedral. Donors of the stained glass windows are named Eschmann and Bauer, a sign of Belleville's ethnic makeup.

Harrison ends at Illinois, where a left will take you to the Public Square.

It is painful to consider that this brutal demonstration of 1970s insensitivity replaced one of the prettiest squares in Illinois. The demolition in 1972 of the 1861 Greek Revival courthouse did have one good effect; it showed the city what happens when a heritage is taken for granted. Belleville formed a Historic Preservation Commission that same year. The city now has historic district zoning, the effects of which will be evident.

Take the first right off the square down Main Street, a happily intact and relatively healthy survivor. Go left on Jackson; its interesting houses include a gray Italianate one with a wrought-iron crown on its tower at 321. Go right on brick-paved East D Street, where 205 stands behind its picket fence.

Go right on Church and follow it a block beyond Main to East Washington; turn left here and admire the extravagantly decorated dwelling at 310, now law offices. A right on Mascoutah takes you a short block to the austere white brick Koerner house. Gustavus Koerner was representative of the people who made Belleville what it is. A graduate in law of Heidelberg University, he got into trouble for taking part in a political demonstration in 1832. He arrived here in 1833, was named to the state supreme court in 1845, served in the legislature then as lieutenant governor in the 1850s. In 1862 Lincoln named him minister to Spain.

Learned immigrants like Koerner were called here, as in Missouri, Latin farmers, because they were more proficient at that language than at growing crops. The botanist George Engelmann, who helped Shaw found his botanical garden in St. Louis, was also from Belleville. The city has the oldest public library in the state.

Continue straight, which means you are on Abend, a street of impressive brick dwellings, mainly Victorian. At the end of the block turn left on Old Cow Street, so called for the cow path it follows. Here are earlier and more humble dwellings, built right on the sidewalk as in Soulard or Hermann, leaving more space for a garden behind. No place in Illinois is more picturesque than Old Cow Street.

Go right a short block on Mascoutah, then right on Fulton, where at 602 is the 1830 Kunz house, the oldest

Greek Revival structure in the state, now a museum open Sundays from 2–4. Note neighboring 600's two stained glass door lights. Continue leftward — the name changes to Survey — and at the end turn left on East Adams, which will return you to Mascoutah. Follow it left several blocks to East Washington.

Belleville's Historical Society occupies fine quarters at 701, which are open to the public, as is its library. Go left on Forest at the end of the street and left again on Main. Follow Main through the Public Square, turning left on Third Street, then right on W. Lincoln and left on Centerville. Centerville takes you to Illinois 15, where a right gives you, after six miles, a choice of routes for St. Louis. Illinois 15 itself is the most direct, taking you through East St. Louis on Missouri Avenue.

More circuitous but interesting is Illinois 157, the Bluff Road which you may follow leftward off Illinois 15 toward Cahokia. It connects to Illinois 163 at a T intersection about a mile beyond Illinois 15; keep to the left on Illinois 157. After a couple of houses on the right you will see a backyard graced by a large gold version of the Statue of Liberty, a patriotic gesture dating from 1976.

Illinois 157 takes you through Cahokia by the Jarrot Mansion and the Church of the Holy Family, where this book began. A right on Illinois 3 returns you by way of Sauget to U.S. 40/Interstate 64, and thence west to St. Louis.

For information call:
Belleville Historical Society 618-234-0600
Cahokia Mounds State Historic Site 618-346-5160
Kunz House 618-234-0600
Shrine of Our Lady of the Snows 618-397-6700

Interpretive Center, Cahokia Mounds State Historic Site

Notes

Chapter 1

[1] Robert de La Salle, letter, *Gazette de France* October 31, 1678.

[2] Governor Ford quoted in Solon J. Buck, *Illinois in 1818* 2nd ed. rev. (Urbana: University of Illinois Press, 1967).

[3] quoted in display case, Cahokia Courthouse.

[4] Nicolas de Finiels, *An Account of Upper Louisiana*, translated by Carl Ekberg, edited by Carl Ekberg and William Foley (Columbia: University of Missouri Press, 1989), p. 82.

[5] Mary Hartwell Catherwood, *Old Kaskaskia*, quoted in Susan Spano Wells, "Louis XV's Mississippi Valley," *New York Times* July 2, 1989.

Chapter 2

[1] Dumont de Montigny, quoted in Carl Ekberg, *Colonial Ste Genevieve* (Gerald: Patrice Press, 1985), p. 305.

[2] Ekberg, *Ste Genevieve*, p. 223.

[3] Ekberg, *Ste Genevieve*, p. 230.

[4] Francis A. Sampson, "Glimpses of Old Missouri by Explorers and Travelers," *Missouri Historical Review*, 68 (1973), p. 87.

[5] Ekberg, *Ste Genevieve*, p. 134.

Chapter 3

[1] William S. Bryan and Robert Rose, *A History of the Pioneer Families of Missouri with Numerous Sketches, Anecdotes, Adventures, etc., Relating to Early Days in Missouri* (St. Louis: Bryan, Brand, 1876), p. 85.

[2] John J. Bagen, *St. Mary of the Barrens Parish: The Early Days* (Perryville: Association of the Miraculous Medal, St. Mary's Seminary, 1987), p. 7.

[3] Bagen, p. 17.

[4] Bagen, p. 25.

[5] Bagen, p. 33.

Chapter 4

[1] *The WPA Guide to 1930s Missouri* (Lawrence: University Press of Kansas, 1986), p. 534, reprint of 1941 edition.

[2] *WPA*, p. 535.

[3] quoted in Forrest Rose, "New View of 'Old Mines'" *Columbia Daily Tribune* October 22, 1989.

[4] Henry Schoolcraft, *A View of the Lead Mines in Missouri* (New York: Charles Wiley and Co., 1819), p. 39.

[5] Schoolcraft, *View*, p. 153.

[6] Schoolcraft, *View*, p. 150.

[7] *WPA*, p. 535.

Chapter 5

[1] Henry Schoolcraft, *A View of the Lead Mines of Missouri* (New York: Charles Wiley and Co., 1819), p. 153.

[2] *The WPA Guide to 1930s Missouri* (Lawrence: University Press of Kansas, 1986), pp. 450-51, reprint of 1941 edition.

[3] Schoolcraft, *View*, p. 91.

[4] Henry Schoolcraft, *Travels in the Central Portion of the Mississippi Valley: Comprising Observations on Its Mineral Geography, Internal Resources, and Aboriginal Population* (New York: Collins and Hannay, 1825), p. 243.

Chapter 6

[1] Jay Monaghan, *Civil War on the Western Border, 1854-1865* (Boston: Little and Brown, 1955), p. 312.

[2] plaque at Fort Davidson—Pilot Knob

[3] plaque at Fort Davidson—Pilot Knob

[4] Leonard Hall, *Stars Upstream: Life Along an Ozark River* (Chicago: University of Chicago Press, 1958), p. 40.

[5] *Missouri Historical Review* (Columbia: State Historical Society, April 1978).

Chapter 8

[1] All Philippine Duchesne quotations are taken from Louise Callan, *Philippine Duchesne, Frontier Missionary of the Sacred Heart, 1769-1852* (Westminster: Newman Press, 1957).

[2] Callan, p. 608.

[3] *The WPA Guide to 1930s Missouri* (Lawrence: University Press of Kansas, 1986), p. 263, reprint of 1941 edition.

[4] *WPA*, p. 265.

Chapter 9

[1] Archibald Henderson, *The Conquest of the Old Southwest* (New York: The Century Co., 1920), p. c.viii.

[2] Lawrence Elliott, *The Long Hunter: A New Life of Daniel Boone* (New York: Reader's Digest Press, 1975).

[3] Commandant of Fort Osage, *Missouri Historical Review* 16 (1921), p. 27, quoted in Elliott, *The Long Hunter*.

[4] Elliott, p. 202.

[5] *The WPA Guide to 1930s Missouri* (Lawrence: University Press of Kansas, 1986), p. 363, reprint of 1941 edition.

[6] *WPA*, p. 363.

[7] Gottfried Duden, *Report on A Journey to the Western States*, general editor, James W. Goodrich, translated and edited by George H.

Kellner, Alfred E. Schroeder, and Wayne Senner (Columbia: State Historical Society of Missouri, 1980), p. 57.

[8] Duden, p. 71.

[9] Duden, p. 57.

[10] Duden, p. 84.

Chapter 10

[1] Anna Hesse and Marion South, *Gasconade County Tours* (1975) was a great help in developing this Hermann itinerary.

[2] Berton Roueché, *Special Places* (Boston: Little and Brown, 1982), p. 66.

Chapter 11

[1] William S. Bryan and Robert Rose, *A History of the Pioneer Families of Missouri with Numerous Sketches, Anecdotes, Adventures, etc., Relating to Early Days in Missouri* (St. Louis: Bryan, Brand, 1876), p. 453.

Chapter 12

[1] Charles Lockwood and Christopher B. Leinberger, "How Business Is Reshaping America," *Atlantic* October 1986, pp. 43-52.

Chapter 13

[1] This driving tour is in part an adaptation of Esley Hamilton's excellent *Hannibal as History*.

Chapter 14

[1] Quoted in E.F. Porter, Jr., "Price of Preservation Challenges Principia," *St. Louis Post-Dispatch* January 21, 1990.

Chapter 15

[1] Washington Irving, "To Catherine Paris." September 13, 1832 quoted in *The Complete Works of Washington Irving*, edited by Ralph M. Aderman, Herbert L. Kleinfield and Jenifer S. Banks (Boston: Twayne Publishers, 1979), vol. 2, p. 723.

[2] Ulysses S. Grant, *Personal Memoirs* (New York: C. L. Webster, 1885-86) , p. 19.

[3] Grant, *Memoirs*, p. 32.

[4] Grant, *Memoirs*, p. 34.

[5] Ulysses S. Grant, *The Papers of Ulysses S. Grant*, edited by John W. Simon, (Carbondale: Southern Illinois University Press, 1967-82), vol. 1, p. 334.

[6] Grant, *Memoirs*, p. 168.

[7] Grant, *Papers*, p. 350.

[8] Bruce Catton, preface, *The Papers of Ulysses S. Grant*, vol. 1, p. xvii.

[9] George McCue, *Sculpture City* (New York: Hudson Hill, 1988), p. 161.

Chapter 16

[1] Kenneth T. Jackson, *Crabgrass Frontier: The Suburbanization of the U.S.* (New York: Oxford University Press, 1985), p. 68.

[2] Calvert Vaux, *Villas and Cottages* quoted in Jackson, p. 67.

[3] William L. Thomas, *History of St. Louis County* (St. Louis: S. J. Clarke Publishing Co., 1911), p. 351.

[4]*Kirkwood Historical Review* (Kirkwood: Kirkwood Historical Society, June 1984).

Chapter 17
[1]Lewis Mumford, *The Culture of Cities* (New York: Harcourt, Brace & Co., 1938), p. 215.
[2]Michael Pollan, "Why Mow? The Case Against Lawns," *The New York Times* May 28, 1989.
[3]Frank J. Scott, *The Art of Beautifying Suburban Home Grounds* (New York: D. Appleton & Co., 1870), p. 61.
[4]Michael Pollan, *The New York Times* May 28, 1989.
[5] Thorstein Veblen, *The Theory of the Leisure Class* (New York: Macmillan, 1912), reprint of 1899 edition.
[6]Lewis Mumford, *The City in History* (New York: Harcourt, Brace & World Inc., 1961), p. 497.
[7]William L. Thomas, *History of St. Louis County* (St. Louis: S. J. Clarke Publishing Co., 1911), p. 76.

Chapter 18
[1]Suzanne Winkler, "A Prehistoric Metropolis in Illinois," *New York Times* September 10, 1989.

Jarrot House, Cahokia

Bibliography

Bagen, John J. *St. Mary of the Barrens Parish: The Early Days*. Perryville: Association of the Miraculous Medal, St. Mary's Seminary, 1987.

Bryan, William S., and Robert Rose. *A History of the Pioneer Families of Missouri, with Numerous Sketches, Anecdotes, Adventures, etc., Relating to Early Days in Missouri*. St. Louis: Bryan, Brand, 1876.

Buck, Solon J. *Illinois in 1818*. 2nd ed. rev. Urbana: University of Illinois Press, 1967.

Callan, Louise. *Philippine Duchesne, Frontier Missionary of the Sacred Heart, 1769-1852*. Westminster: Newman Press, 1957.

Catton, Bruce. Preface. *The Papers of Ulysses S. Grant*. By Ulysses S. Grant. Edited by John W. Simon. Carbondale, Ill.: Southern Illinois University Press, 1967-82. Vol. 1.

The Complete Works of Washington Irving. Edited by Ralph M. Aderman, Herbert L. Kleinfield, and Jenifer S. Banks. Boston: Twayne Publishers, 1979. Vol. 2.

Davis, Norah D. *The Father of Waters*. San Francisco: Sierra Club, 1982.

de Finiels, Nicolas. *An Account of Upper Louisiana*. Translated by Carl Ekberg. Edited by Carl Ekberg and William Foley. Columbia: University of Missouri Press, 1989.

Duden, Gottfried. *Report on A Journey to the Western States of North America and a Stay of Several Years Along the Missouri (during the years 1824, '25, '26, and 1827)*. General Editor James W. Goodrich. Translated and Edited by George H. Kellner, Alfred E. Schroeder, and Wayne Senner. Columbia: State Historical Society of Missouri, 1980.

Ekberg, Carl J. *Colonial Ste Genevieve*. Gerald: Patrice Press, 1985.

Elliott, Lawrence. *The Long Hunter: A New Life of Daniel Boone*. New York: Reader's Digest Press, 1975.

Faherty, William B. *Dream by the River: Two Centuries of St. Louis Catholicism, 1766-1967*. 2nd ed. rev. St. Louis: Piraeus, 1981.

Grant, Ulysses S. *The Papers of Ulysses S. Grant*. Edited by John W. Simon. Carbondale, Ill.: Southern Illinois University Press, 1967-82. Vol. 1.

——. *Personal Memoirs*. New York: C. L. Webster, 1885-86. Vol. 1.

Hall, Leonard. *Stars Upstream: Life Along an Ozark River*. Chicago: University of Chicago Press, 1958.

Hamilton, Esley. *Hannibal as History*. Hannibal: 1975.

Henderson, Archibald. *The Conquest of the Old Southwest: The Romantic Story of the Early Pioneers into Virginia, the Carolinas, Tennessee and Kentucky, 1740-1790*. New York: The Century Co., 1920.

Hesse, Anna, and Marion South. *Gasconade County Tours*. 1975.

Jackson, Kenneth. *Crabgrass Frontier: The Suburbanization of the U.S.* New York: Oxford University Press, 1985.

Kirkwood Historical Review (Kirkwood: Kirkwood Historical Society, June 1984).

La Salle, Robert de. Letter. *Gazette de France* . 31 Oct. 1678.

Lockwood, Charles, and Christopher B. Leinberger. "How Business is Reshaping America." *Atlantic* October 1986, pp. 43-52.

McCue, George. *Sculpture City*. New York: Hudson Hill, 1988.

Missouri Historical Review (Columbia: State Historical Society, April 1978).

Monaghan, Jay. *Civil War on the Western Border 1854-1985*. Boston: Little and Brown, 1955.

Mumford, Lewis. *The City in History*. New York: Harcourt, Brace & World, 1961.

Mumford, Lewis. *The Culture of Cities*. New York: Harcourt, Brace & Co., 1938.

Pollan, Michael. "Why Mow? The Case Against Lawns." *New York Times* 28 May 1989, C4+.

Porter, E.F., Jr. "Price of Preservation Challenges Principia." *St. Louis Post-Dispatch* 21 Jan. 1990, C4+.

Rose, Forrest. "New View of 'Old Mines.' " *Columbia Daily Tribune* 22 Oct. 1989.

Roueché, Berton. *Special Places*. Boston: Little and Brown, 1982.

Sampson, Francis A. "Glimpses of Old Missouri by Explorers and Travelers." 1907. *Missouri Historical Review* 68 (1973), pp. 74-93.

Schoolcraft, Henry. *Travels in the Central Portion of the Mississippi Valley: Comprising Observations on Its Mineral Geography, Internal Resources, and Aboriginal Population*. New York: Collins and Hannay, 1825.

———. *A View of the Lead Mines of Missouri*. New York: Charles Wiley and Co., 1819.

Scott, Frank J. *The Art of Beautifying Suburban Home Grounds*. New York: D. Appleton & Co., 1870.

Thomas, William L. *History of St. Louis County*. St. Louis: S. J. Clarke Publishing Co., 1911.

Veblen, Thorstein. *The Theory of the Leisure Class*. New York: Macmillan, 1912.

The WPA Guide to 1930s Missouri. Lawrence: University Press of Kansas, 1986. Reprint of 1941 edition.

Wells, Susan Spano. "Louis XV's Mississippi Valley." *New York Times* 2 Jul. 1989, pp. 8-9+.

Winkler, Suzanne. "A Prehistoric Metropolis in Illinois." *New York Times* 10 Sept. 1989, section 5, p. 19+.

Index

215

Design: Louise Daugherty
Maps: Kimberly Shotten

Bolduc House, Ste Genevieve

Barringer Fifield was graduated in history from Stanford University and received a doctorate in political science from the University of Rome. He is the author of *Seeing Saint Louis*, a guide to the city and its characteristic neighborhoods.

Keith Recker studied poetry and French at Carnegie-Mellon University and American literature at the University of Michigan. He is currently writing a guide to Pittsburgh with Barringer Fifield.

Herb Weitman, director of photographic services and an adjunct professor in the School of Fine Arts at Washington University, is nationally recognized for his work in editorial photography. His work is represented in a number of museums and private collections.

221